In the Palm of His Hand

My Journey of Faith

KATHLEEN A. FRENCH

ISBN 978-1-68197-549-8 (paperback)
ISBN 978-1-68197-550-4 (digital)

Copyright © 2016 by Kathleen French
All rights reserved. No part of this publication may be reproduced, distributed, or transmitted in any form or by any means, including photocopying, recording, or other electronic or mechanical methods without the prior written permission of the publisher. For permission requests, solicit the publisher via the address below.

Christian Faith Publishing, Inc.
296 Chestnut Street
Meadville, PA 16335
www.christianfaithpublishing.com

Printed in the United States of America

To my children, Todd and Emily, in the hopes that they will remember their grandma Busse with love and understand their mother and my journey of faith through life's challenges.

There comes a time in life
When your world stands still.
You face nothing but tears and strife
And life's value is at nil.
But over the hill is a beam
Of sunlight bright and gay.
And happiness so it seems
Has arrived at a latter day.
Keep thinking right will win
And love will find away.
To heal the wounds of sin
That blight our life so grey.

— Dorothy Kenney Busse

Biography

My mother was born on a summer day in Chicago on June 19, 1910. She was named Dorothy Marie by her parents, James Joseph Sr. and Mary Ellen Kenney. Her father was of Irish Catholic descent, and her mother was a Scottish Presbyterian who later in life converted to Catholicism. The Kenney family consisted of five children, Dorothy, Jack, Jim, George, and Eleanor, who died at the age of eighteen months from a bout with pertussis. The Kenney family moved to Joliet around 1922 during the First World War. Dorothy and her brothers attended Saint Patrick's grade school. Dorothy excelled as a beautiful soprano singer at St. Patrick's and became Monsignor Kennedy's favorite singer. He requested that my mother sing a particular favorite of his at the graduation exercises. I often remember my mother telling me that he spoke with a deep Irish drawl saying, "I want Dorothy to sing the 'Panis Angelicus,'" and she did.

Dorothy went on to attend Saint Francis Academy in Joliet, which was located at Wilcox and Taylor Streets. The former academy now is the home of the University of Saint Francis. Dorothy was a member of the graduating class of 1929. During her time at the academy, Dorothy received numerous awards for her penmanship from the Palmer Institute of Writing. Among her talents were, not only her love of singing, but her love of poetry as well. She wrote many poems, but apparently she never kept them in any sort of journal. One piece that she authored was titled "School-Days Sunset," and it read like this:

> The sunset of our school days
> Is fast approaching near.
> But if we heed St. Francis' ways
> We need have naught to fear.
> (chorus)
> For our colors green and gold,
> On the highest peg we'll pin.
> To *Quo Vadis*, our motto, we'll hold
> While endeavoring to win.
> As we journey down life's way
> And are striving for the prize
> O! Alma Mater, SFA,
> To glory you'll bid us rise.
> The curtain is about to fall
> On the class of twenty-nine.
> Teachers, classmates, one and all,
> Wish us well in our new line.
>
> Dorothy M. Kenney

Dorothy was a cheerleader for Saint Francis, and among her personal effects that were found after her death was her sweater emblem from that SFA. Perhaps, the above poem was written more as a cheer or a song.

Strangely enough, Mom dreamt of being employed as an office manager in charge over a large office, perhaps in Chicago. She loved bookkeeping and excelled in her secretarial skills. However, during her last year of school, Dorothy became seriously ill with scarlet fever and almost died. As a result, she felt that she lost her sense of rhythm because she could no longer write her poetry as well or sing in her beautiful soprano voice. During her illness, her path took a different turn, away from her chosen field of business to a career in nursing. She desired to repay her debt to the Lord for sparing her life and felt that nursing was her way to do this. She entered into Saint Joseph's School of Nursing in the fall of 1931 during the height of the Great Depression. Money was a scarce commodity, so Dorothy worked during her schooling as a nursing assistant to help defray the cost of her room and board at the school. The students were given a monthly allotment of five dollars for their personal use.

Among her classmates at Saint Joseph's was Sister Therese Ettelbrick, who would later rise to the position of hospital administrator at Saint Joseph Hospital, where Dorothy was later employed.

Dorothy met and married Theodore Busse in the spring of 1941 when they eloped to Mexico, Missouri. Shortly after they married, Ted was drafted into the army to play his part in World War II. They were separated for a period of forty-two months, during which time Dorothy continued to work in her field of nursing at Little Company of Mary Hospital in Chicago. Dorothy and Ted corresponded frequently during their separation and would often write poetry to one another. Several poems were found from this time. The following selections are from one of each of Dorothy's and Ted's to each other.

My Dream

I dream of days we'll be together
I dream of times you'll leave me never.
I dream our love grows deeper, better.
I dream these dreams though storm clouds gather.
I know my love will be back soon.

I know we'll bask 'neath light of moon.
I know if home be just one room,
I know we'll win what ere our doom.
I want success for both we two.
I want our skies all tinged with blue.
I want a son to be like you,
I want your love, indeed I do.

Dorothy Busse

Ted wrote back with these lines.

Soon the years will fly
And we won't hear people cry
For the loved ones lost and left behind.
We shall all have time to rest
In our heavenly home on high
And feel stronger by the hour
Resting our heads against Jesus' breast.

Ted Busse

The war brought many hardships and trials to their marriage. They tried their best to endure. On May 7, 1989, Ted and Dorothy would have celebrated their forty-eighth wedding anniversary. Together they raised two sons, John and Douglas, and a daughter, Kathleen.

Dorothy was best remembered for her compassion and wit. She enjoyed life despite the trials she endured. Her heart went out to the less fortunate and those who might have just needed a friend. Another verse that I found after her death included a little verse which sums up what I believe she felt her purpose in life to be. It is titled "Let Me Give."

IN THE PALM OF HIS HAND: MY JOURNEY OF FAITH

I do not know how long I'll live,
But while I live, Lord, let me give
Some comfort to someone in need
By smile or nod, kind word or deed.
And let me do what e'er I can
To ease things for my fellow man.
I want naught but to do my part
To "lift" a tired or weary heart.
To change folks frowns to smiles again—
Then I will not have lived in vain.
And I'll care not how long I'll live
If I can give and give and give.

Dorothy Kenney Busse gave of herself and never asked anything in return except the love of God and her family. Surely, she had that and more from her family and many, many dear friends to whom this book is dedicated with love.

Kathleen French

Prologue

My mother was forty-two years old when I was born. She often told me of the joy that she felt at my birth. She was overjoyed at the idea of her motherhood, which began at the age of thirty-seven with the birth of my oldest brother, John, followed thirteen months later with the birth her second son and completed at the age of forty-two when I was born. She had four pregnancies, one which resulted in a miscarriage between my brother Doug and me. She said that my dad was convinced the other child was a girl too even though the pregnancy terminated too soon to tell. We always let Dad assume that he was right. Dad liked to believe that they would have two boys and two girls, a nice even number and demonstrative of a good Catholic family. My mother was grateful to have any children, let alone three healthy babies like she had. I often wished that I could have had a sister, especially now, but I have dear friends and two wonderful sisters-in-law that have shared my life as though we were true sisters.

When I was born, Mom asked God to grant her one small prayer request, that she would live long enough to get me through high school. Her prayers were answered. She lived to a splendid age of seventy-eight years, halfway to seventy-nine. Years that were sometimes difficult, but basically good years.

She saw to it that I had many wonderful experiences throughout my childhood, which left me with many wonderful memories. I enjoyed ballet and tap dance lessons given by a wonderful lady who taught them in a mysteriously secretive dance studio atop her three-story brick house. My brothers had memories too, of baseball and scouting. John even went all the way to Eagle Scout There were memories of summers spent at the summer cottage of Dad's uncle on Pell Lake in Wisconsin, of family reunions, of neighborhood parties, of roller- and ice-skating—in other words, a normal, happy childhood, despite my parent's late start in parenting due to their separation during World War II.

I remember attending kindergarten at the public school where I excelled in hat and shoe tying. My teacher was a very special lady who had the patience of a saint. She was fond of my mother and even attended her wake when she died.

I was in Brownies and Girl Scouts. I enjoyed the many activities; and my mother wanted to do her best despite being an older mom. I thought she was just wonderful.

I remember how much I hated it when someone referred to her as my grandmother, which happened several times because she had a beautiful head of white hair which led people to believe she was too old to be my mom. I would quickly correct the error, telling the offender that my grandmother had grey hair, and her name was Mrs. Kenney. It seemed to me as a child that I had to defend my mother's honor.

Our mother-daughter relationship was not perfect. We had our ups and downs, but we became good friends over the years, and I believe that is how our story evolved. I was her comforter in the days of dark times. We shared a special relationship, one that spanned my entire thirty-six years. Sometimes, perhaps, we were too close. I

IN THE PALM OF HIS HAND: MY JOURNEY OF FAITH

was between her and my dad. She confided in me many things that should have been confided in her husband, but she was not able to communicate well with him. I am not saying that this was right, but I became her shoulder—and her strength. During my teenage years, we grew apart. I guess this is normal. I'm sure she cried, and I know she prayed for me many times over. She continued to pray for me throughout my teen years and into my twenties. When she retired, due to her failing health, from her medical profession of nursing, I bore her grief with her that she endured from a retirement that she did not want. I shared in the burden it placed on her emotionally, even though it placed a sometimes unbearable grief on me.

When I approached the time of my marriage, we grew closer once again, sharing happy memories of all the planning and preparation of the upcoming marital event. Although she had always hoped that I would marry in the Catholic Church, she accepted it when I told her that I was not going to be able to have the ceremony in the Catholic Church due to circumstances that I could not control or change at that time. She was, nonetheless, supportive of my decision and stood by me all the way. Besides, she was very fond of Ernie, my future husband. I am so grateful for that.

Thus it was with mom and me. I thought she was the tower of strength. I thought she would live forever, like her mother who lived to the astonishing age of ninety-seven. I believe, though, that when her mother died that twenty-second day in July of 1987, the rubber band snapped inside. Her spirit, her zest for life, diminished. What followed was the deterioration of her health, which is where our story begins.

Spring 1988

My mother was dying, yet we could not determine why. She had been in the hospital twice so far that year. No conclusions had been drawn, and she continued to slide further down. We did have a small reprieve, a miracle of sorts, back in April. She was showing signs of blood in her lower intestinal tract, and of course, we feared the worst—cancer.

I persuaded Mom to attend a healing Mass with Father Kelleher from the Marian Healing Ministry in Brooklyn, New York, at St. Dennis Church in Lockport, Illinois. I took Mom there in a wheelchair, and she was given priority seating in the front of the church. The church was very crowded with people coming from miles around, seeking a miracle in their lives or just observing, to judge whether this was truly a genuine experience or just someone's idea of a hoax. The church was filled to capacity, and the overflow was seated downstairs. In fact, I was told that I would have to go downstairs to the basement and watch the Mass on a large projector screen. Instinctively, I felt that this would not do. I recognized a woman who was acting as a hostess for this Mass and asked her if there was any possibility of sitting upstairs in the church itself. She looked around and suggested that I check out the side aisle where I might find a seat for one person. As luck would have it, I spotted a seat just one row behind a dear friend from our church. I left my belongings there and walked up to the front of the church to assure Mom that I was nearby in case she needed me. The services were very special to me, as this was the second healing Mass Mom and I attended together, and my pastor was also going to be a part of this particular celebration.

Father Kelleher spoke about healing and how sometimes it took more than one healing Mass, or more than one prayer to God for intervention. In other words, it would take patience, a virtue that I sometimes felt I greatly lacked in my personal life.

He also suggested that a person who needed healing might want to look around the church that evening, or think of a friend or loved one not present, who perhaps might need a miracle more than one-self. He suggested that we might try praying for that person's needs rather than our own which may surprise us by actually healing us through another's intercession. Father Kelleher went on to relate a story of an older man with horrible back pain, a pain so intense that he could not stand upright, who had attended one of his healing Masses. That night he was the last one to receive the blessing from Father Kelleher. While he was patiently waiting for his turn up at the altar, he prayed fervently for others he saw at that church who he felt needed help more than himself. He went home after he was blessed, not feeling any particular difference, but more at peace with himself. Two days later, he phoned the ministry office in New York with such excitement that he could not contain his enthusiasm. He told the secretary that he had been healed!

His pain which he had suffered for so many years was completely gone! He had never once asked the Lord to heal him. That night, I prayed for two special people in my life: for my mother, that we may find the problem or cure, and for my sister-in-law who had

IN THE PALM OF HIS HAND: MY JOURNEY OF FAITH

been stricken with multiple sclerosis, forcing her to use a wheelchair at all times.

I remember going up to the front of the church after the Mass, to await the blessing service, the healing part of the gathering. That night my mom looked especially lovely, dressed in a two-piece navy-blue suit, accented by a pretty peach-colored blouse. She sat, waiting apprehensively for the priests to start the blessing service. As they emerged from the sacristy, they moved down the row of people seated in wheelchairs. Soon Mom was blessed by three of the five priests in attendance that night, including my own pastor who took time to pray with Mom for her special needs. Although Mom was especially fond of my pastor, Father Ted, she had so hoped to be blessed by Father Kelleher himself. Suddenly it was as if he had appeared out of nowhere; my mother was surrounded by the tall figure of Father Kelleher.

He placed her chin on his hand, and she smiled with her Irish eyes. He spoke softly and told her that she had the most beautiful smile. My mother told him that no one had ever "accused" her of having a beautiful anything. He just smiled and asked her what she was asking the Lord to do for her that night. Immediately, she spoke of the needs of my sister-in-law with MS and of a dear friend's husband who had colon cancer. Father Kelleher smiled again and said that she indeed would be blessed that night. He kissed her gently on her forehead and moved on. Mom was overwhelmed and felt limp, but yet another priest moved toward her and blessed her. The evening was a wonderfully rewarding one, one of faith shared by so many and especially one shared by my mother and her daughter. The drive home was quiet. My thoughts were still focusing on the events of the evening. I felt God's presence was with us, and I held on to the hope that there would be a miracle in our lives. Mom kissed me good-bye when we returned to their house, and thanked me for taking her to the service. She promised to call me in the morning. I assured her that she was going to be all right because these feelings that I had were too strong to be mistaken. I was expecting a miracle!

The next day Mom was not well at all, and it seemed as though the Mass was a waste of our time. However Mom felt that there was a reason to all of this and that we would soon get the answer. She was beaming over the thought of the entire Mass. It had made a very special impression on her. I think she secretly enjoyed it when Father referred to her beautiful smile. It was a shame that she never thought of herself as being a beautiful person.

When I think of my own childhood, I recall that I, too, never felt that I was a beautiful person. I'm sure my mom must have told me somewhere along the span of my childhood that I was beautiful, but perhaps she stopped telling me too soon. I hope that if I get one message across to my children, it will be that they are beautiful, not only in the physical sense, but from the inside, in their spiritual sense. I hope that they grow up with confidence and high self-esteem to spare them the painful experiences that I went through growing up without confidence in myself or in what I had to offer as an individual.

I spoke to my sister-in-law Darlene that day and asked her how she felt. She said she experienced a great surge in her energy level, that her strength seemed greater than it had in a very long time. I told her about the Mass, and she was full of wonder. She said she hoped that Mom would be feeling better soon, and we ended our conversation on that positive note.

Darlene is probably one of my best friends. It is unfortunate that she lives so far away because we have such a friendship that we seem in tune to each other's emotional moods. We can cry together and laugh together, all in the span of an hour's conversation. She knows my many insecurities and thoughts that I cannot share with anyone; but with her I can express my thoughts easily, and there is no judgment made—she just listens. My greatest prayer for her is one

IN THE PALM OF HIS HAND: MY JOURNEY OF FAITH

of happiness amidst the awful confusion in her life since the divorce from my brother. I was afraid that the friendship that we shared for fourteen years of her marriage might end when she divorced, but the good Lord knew I needed to share that time with her, and it had strengthened my faith as a result. We had been through many periods of darkness after her divorce, and it would have been easy to fall into a great vat of depression, but I made the choice to be an encouragement to my dear friend, and as a result both she and I had learned to trust our Lord with every facet of our lives.

When I feel temptation looming over me, I turn to our Lord and ask Him to reveal to me the purpose of this trial. Invariably He shows me what it is that He wishes me to do. I don't always realize it as soon as I should, but when I finally find the reason, it makes that decision easier to bear.

Saturday arrived, and my mom called me with great excitement. Her bleeding had stopped! She felt better than she had in a very long time. On Monday, she walked into the doctor's office, where only a week before she had been brought in a wheelchair. She even shared the news or the healing Mass with her physician, and he listened intently. She was praising God and witnessing to all who would hear.

Her behavior was reminiscent of the period in my life in the early '70s when I joined the Jesus People movement in my local community. I was out to save the whole world! I told everyone about the salvation of the Lord, and attended many different churches trying to find the one with the "answer." My poor mother was not even spared from my enthusiasm. I even questioned her faith! I thought I knew it all—after all, I had been saved! It took me a long time to realize that I had missed the one single most important message that our Lord had wanted His people to hear, that is, that we should love one another the same way that He has loved us, just where we are without any stipulations.

Some people of God tend to put on the conditions, meaning that we tend to set down a list of rules in order for us to be worthy to be in God's presence. I found out much later that no matter what I think about the person next to me, whether he practices his faith the way I think he should, God loves him just the way he is. I am sure that this revelation came through the efforts of my mother's unceasing prayers for me. I left the movement after I found there were things going on that in my heart I knew were not right. Now I was witnessing the effects of the healing Mass on my mother and watching her faith be "born again" as she shared the good news of the healing that she received through divine intercession and prayer.

The following Wednesday evening, my son's graduation from kindergarten religious education class arrived, and Grandma and Grandpa could not miss this important event. Mom walked in and eagerly shared the wonderful news of her healing to all who would listen, including our pastor and both of the nuns at our parish. They listened as she spoke of the wonderful news, and told her how happy they were for her, even though I wondered if they truly believed that a healing had indeed taken place.

A few weeks later a strange thing happened. The husband of a close friend of my mother's was in Mayo Clinic awaiting surgery on his colon. He had taken a turn for the worse and was doing so poorly that they couldn't operate until his condition improved. The woman was afraid that her husband would die. My mother offered, in her prayers to God, to share a part of the miracle she had received so that this man could get better. He improved, but my mother started to decline once more. Never once, though, did Mom complain or curse God. She was grateful that the man had improved. Her loss of health was worth it to her for his improvement, but she was growing weary from being very sick.

August 1988

After several weeks of nausea and the inability to eat anything nourishing, Mom had to go in the hospital for the third time. Her doctor decided that a surgeon should examine the lining of the stomach wall to see if there was something inside causing her problem. The procedure was simple enough but very uncomfortable for a seventy-eight-year-old woman in such a weakened state. As the procedure took place, I stood waiting in the hallway with my father, praying that the results would be good. Maybe just a simple medication adjustment would be the answer. The findings were encouraging. The surgeon seemed to think that the medication that Mom was on for polymyalgia rheumatica (PMR), a disease that causes severe pain in the muscles, had ulcerated the lining of the stomach wall. We breathed a sigh of relief when he said it was not cancer. Her specialist who prescribed that medication was called in to consult and change it. We were hoping that changing the medication to a less stressful one would enable her to resume normal eating patterns and thus regain her appetite and put on the weight she had lost. She came home in a couple of days, though she was still not well, and continued to get thinner as the days wore on. The nausea had taken its toll. Mom had gone from a weight of 134 pounds in January of 1988, to a mere 112 pounds at this point. She felt she was dying a little each day. She called her sons home. My older brother, John; his wife, Kathy Kay; and their daughter, Stacie, came in from Colorado and stayed with us. Our folks thought it would be easier on them since Mom did not sleep well, often being up all night with nausea.

My children were thrilled. This was a chance for the cousins to share some special time together. It was a great benefit to me, as it allowed my brother and me, separated by an age span of five years and by many miles, to come to a better understanding of each other. We were never really close, as he was grown and out of the house by the time I reached my teenage years.

John left home at the age of nineteen to join the Unite States Air Force. We were never near each other until he moved back to Illinois for a period of five years, which came to an end in August 1987, when it became clear that he would once again be moving out of state due to his job.

My brother Doug came in at this time also, but we did not see each other because our lives were separated by his divorce from my sister-in-law Darlene. He came for my mother, and that was what was important at the time. My mother's brother, George, and his wife, Ginny, from California also came to town as was their custom at this time of year. In the past we would have had a gala celebration for my grandmother's birthday, but she passed away a year ago on July 22, 1987.

My aunt and uncle came to our house for an intimate dinner with my parents and my family. They shared some laughs and pleasant conversation. Mom was a frail figure of about 105 pounds by now and had somehow grown to resemble her own mother, who lived to the age of ninety-seven. As my aunt and uncle were getting ready to leave, we shared some private thoughts. Each of us knew that Mom was failing and that this could well be the last visit they

IN THE PALM OF HIS HAND: MY JOURNEY OF FAITH

would have with her. I fought back the tears, kissed them good-bye, and watched as their car drove out of sight. I wondered if they truly thought of this as their last time together. If so, I wondered what special moment would be remembered most.

Tuesday, September 27

Mom was not well at all. Two weeks ago, she had gone to the doctor, complaining of pain in her side. There was a visible lump which the doctor dismissed as a pulled muscle. When the pain became too intense, Mom made an appointment to visit her specialist who was treating the PMR disease. He was horrified by the size of the growth in her abdomen and immediately had the nurse order a scan to be done the following day. He notified her regular physician that this was to be done, and her doctor took over on the orders. Mom was very upset. I was furious that her doctor overlooked the first visible sign we had been given to pinpoint her illness.

    I sensed that she was very weary from all the trips to the doctors. Mom was very upset that her own physician had ignored her symptoms and did not look into the matter when she had been to see him two weeks before. I asked her if she wanted to speak to him about it, but she told me that she was too tired to argue with him. I offered to call and talk to him for her, and she told me to go ahead.

    I called her doctor and raised a few questions to him as to why he had overlooked her symptoms. He tried to calm me down, but I was extremely upset at the lack of concern he had shown my mother.

IN THE PALM OF HIS HAND: MY JOURNEY OF FAITH

I told him to inform me personally of the scan results, adding that this was with the approval of my mom. I also felt he owed my mother an apology for not paying attention to her condition and ordering a scan himself. He said he was very sorry and promised to call my mother. If it were not for the fact that my mother was also a professional person, perhaps I could dismiss her behavior as an overreaction, but she had been a nurse for over forty years and held a great respect for the medical profession. When the doctor called my mother, he did not actually apologize, but he did assure her that he would obtain the scan results as soon as possible.

Friday, September 30

The results of the scan came back today. The growth appeared to be large, possibly attached to the gall bladder. Her doctor scheduled an appointment with a surgeon from the medical group for the following Monday. We kept our fears to ourselves, but each of us prayed very fervently that weekend that our deepest fears would not become a reality. We went about our business in a somewhat normal state, but I did promise my mother that I would be there at the surgeon's office at the appointed time to show her my support. She and I shared a special relationship that way. We were there for each other, no matter what. Even when we disagreed, we always tried to keep our perspective. We were not just mother and daughter. We were friends.

Monday, October 3

Mom and Dad met my daughter, Emily, and me at the surgeon's office. After the surgeon entered the examining room, he introduced himself and proved to be a soft-spoken person. He listened intently as my mother reviewed the past year with all its ups and downs in her physical being. He inquired about the pain in her abdomen and asked her how intense it was. She confirmed that the pain was indeed great and that she did not think she could stand it much longer.

When she finished, he quietly closed her medical file and gave us his summation of her condition. Although he sympathized with her weakened state, he said that there appeared to be no other alternative but to surgically remove the growth that was causing her such immense pain. My eyes filled up with tears. I was scared to have her undergo surgery in her present condition, but I knew that she could not continue on this way.

The doctor said that he wanted to schedule surgery for the following Friday and told her that she should go straight to the hospital to be admitted. Mom refused, saying that she would go in the next day, as she needed time to call her family, her sons, her brothers, and her sister-in-law. My daughter and I left to go shopping for new pajamas for my mother for this trip to the hospital. This was the fourth trip to the hospital this year, and no matter what, she wanted time to prepare. New pajamas gave her a sense of hope, a hope that perhaps this time would not be as difficult as we had anticipated.

At the mall Mom's small size was not that easy to find, and the selection was very limited. I was in a hurry, as usual. I had to be home to meet my son's three-thirty school bus. The tears were spilling down my face, and Emily asked me why I was crying. "Are you crying about your mother?" she inquired in a compassionate way well beyond her young years.

"Yes," I replied. "Your grandma is very sick."

Thoughts raced through my mind. This was Monday, surgery on Friday. My mother might *die* on Friday. What if the surgery was too intense for her? The thought of my mother dying tore through me like a knife. I choked back the tears, paid for my selections, and raced back to my mother's house. I helped her pack her bag for the trip to the hospital. Mom and Dad were picking at each other, making unkind remarks, an obvious sign of the stress that they felt but were unable to talk about. I couldn't stand it any longer. I snapped at them and told them that it might make more sense to expend their energy on loving each other rather than fighting each other. So my dad responded by saying to Mom, "I love you," in a deep, gruff voice. I poked my mother on the elbow. "I love you, too," she replied sweetly. I encouraged them to say that to each other every day, assuring them that it would indeed make them feel so much better.

I hated to leave, but I had to get home to my family. My son, Todd, was waiting for me at the neighbor's house, and my husband was due home from work soon. We said our good-byes and left, assuring each other that we would pray for God's intervention once more. I hugged my mom tightly, wishing I could always know that feeling of her hug around my shoulders. On the way home, I cried. I cried for myself because I could lose my best friend, and for my chil-

IN THE PALM OF HIS HAND: MY JOURNEY OF FAITH

dren, who may grow up without knowing my mother's love. I cried for my mother, wishing she did not have to go through all of this.

The thought of my children not having their grandma near to love them and share their lives was a difficult thought to deal with. To me, a grandma's love is a very special love. Our children's other grandma lived three hours away, so it was not going to be easy for the children not having a grandma nearby.

The night seemed long. The tasks of preparing the children for bed seemed to drag on for hours. I'm sure they sensed my discomfort and reacted to that stress. My prayers that night were prayers of pleading—to please make my mother well—as I'm not ready to lose her yet.

Tuesday, October 4

Mom entered the hospital in the morning. The doctors had orders for a complete status report on her condition prior to the scheduled surgery. At this point surgery was still scheduled for Friday, October 7. Mom had made all her phone calls the night before to all her family. My older brother, John, decided to fly in the night before surgery to provide Mom with as much moral support as we could muster. I was grateful that I would not have to be the only child present with Mom as we faced the possibilities of the unknown. I tried to assure Mom that no matter what the outcome was that we would face it together as we had faced so many things together in the past. It was not easy to conceal my worst fears, but I knew that I had to be a positive influence for her sake.

I looked forward to seeing my brother John again in such a short period of time. Our visit in August was mutually rewarding. We found that we both shared many of the same concerns over our family's lives and that even though we were separated by the miles, we could be close in our hearts. It was an intimate time of rediscovery, finding out that we both had traveled down the same roads, suffering many of the emotional wounds and, surprisingly, emerged to

IN THE PALM OF HIS HAND: MY JOURNEY OF FAITH

face the challenges of life with more confidence and self-esteem than we ever thought we possessed. I think I owe my mother a great deal of thanks for that because she constantly prayed for her children, as all good mothers should. Even when left my church for several years, she never criticized me or disowned me. Rather, she just prayed even harder. When my brother John returned to church, she was jubilant. He returned for his own reasons, and when his wife joined the Catholic Church, I believe this made their relationship closer.

I had decided to return to my church when my prayers were answered by my becoming pregnant with our first child. I had tried without any success to become pregnant, going so far as to consider taking a drug to help me become pregnant. Eventually, I was led to the University of Illinois Obstetrics and Gynecology Department, where I was treated by a doctor who showed great understanding and respect. He sympathized with my dilemma and offered to try other ideas before resorting to drug therapy.

Thankfully, the strategy he worked out proved successful, and I discovered that I was carrying a child just after the Christmas of 1981. I am sure that my mother had been praying for that need also, as she knew how much I wanted to have a child.

It was during the time of my pregnancy that I made the decision to return to my roots, to my childhood faith, so I sought out the local Catholic church. Upon that decision, many things in my life changed. I became a churchgoer once again, with a fresh look at my faith and a deeper understanding of what church meant to me. I used to complain that the only thing the church wanted was *money*, but since becoming an adult and having to budget my husband's paycheck, I realized that it was not easy to stretch the money coming in to cover all the expenses going out. Becoming a parent made me realize that maybe my parents had not done such a bad job after all. They were just like us, struggling to know what decisions were right for the whole family in all areas, including education. I went through eight years of a solid Catholic schooling which probably was of great benefit to me as it provided me with a deeper understanding of my faith, which is probably why I chose to return to my church before our son Todd was born. I remember Mom's excitement at the news that I had decided to rejoin my church and have our son baptized Catholic. She was thrilled; her prayers had been answered.

As I gazed into my mother's face, knowing that this could very well be our last days together, I resolved to tell her thank you for being such a great mom. I had been telling her in many ways over the last months of her illness, but I decided to make it clear to her just how much her love had meant to me through all my years. She smiled at me with that beautiful Irish smile and told me not to worry—everything would be okay. She was at peace with God, willing to accept His will no matter what that might entail. I hoped I could be as firm in my faith when I would be put to that test. It always seems easy to say "Trust in God," but sometimes it is not always that simple to let Him have total control and to accept the outcome.

Wednesday, October 5

The tests showed that Mom's blood workup and electrolytes were not stable. They put her on IV therapy to help balance her electrolytes and also started her on antibiotics to ward off any secondary infections. The doctors conferred and decided to postpone surgery until the first of the week to allow the therapy to help boost Mom's physical condition, thus providing a stronger chance of surviving the surgery. I had suspicions that her electrolytes might be off as she had become easily confused and not in complete control. This was extremely frustrating for her because she knew it was happening. Surgery was rescheduled for Tuesday, October 11, at 10:30 a.m. My brother changed his arrival to Monday afternoon. The rest of the week was spent trying to boost her morale with the hope of giving her a sense of inner strength and peace. The surgery was officially titled a gallbladder removal. It sounded simple enough—go in and remove the troublesome organ and all would be well. Or would it?

Monday, October 10

Monday arrived, and I went up to the hospital to see both Mom and John. We exchanged hugs and kisses and conversed about our children and all the things they were into. My visit with Mom was nice, but still the thoughts of her dying loomed overhead. I was more scared than ever in my life to think that this could be our last time together. We hadn't talked much about the outcome before, but now Mom earnestly addressed what I was sure she knew was foremost in both of our minds. Cancer. Somehow the word itself is a death sentence. What if…? I assured her that no matter what we'd cross that bridge when we got there. She resigned that fear with a sense of peace. All the while I was praying that the Lord would spare her the suffering she might have to endure. As much as I loved my mother, I did not want to see her suffer. The thoughts were not pleasant. I left for home with a heavy heart. I cried myself to sleep and waited for morning to come.

Tuesday, October 11

We arrived promptly at the hospital. I had dropped Emily off at my good friend Pat's house. How often I had relied on her help to keep my kids this past year during numerous trips to the hospital for my mom. She was always more than willing to care for my daughter. She had a daughter three months younger than Emily. They got along very well. Pat and I had met one day at the back of church. We each had our two children in tow, attempting to keep them quiet so that we could hear the Mass. We often laughed at the benefits of bringing ourselves and our children to church. Did we really gain anything? Sometimes we weren't sure. From that chance meeting that the Lord arranged developed a great friendship and inspired us to launch a Sunday mother's babysitting club.

There had been babysitting services before, but they were not completely reliable. We decided to try a program of our own. After much discussion, we launched it on Easter Sunday morning, 1987. Pat and I took the challenge in hand and felt we could handle anything that might come our way. It was a success, but the first few minutes were a total panic, as mothers brought in their babies, toddlers, and young children. The enthusiasm was tremendous, and volunteers began signing up for their turn on a Sunday. We were thrilled. I had firsthand evidence that the Lord truly blesses efforts when He is the inspiration.

What a long way we have come since that day. We were now looking toward our second anniversary on Easter 1989. It still amazes me how much cooperation we had received. Now I was depending on my good friend and partner Pat to help me care for my daughter on what could be my mother's last day of life.

The nurses were busy preparing things for the surgery. I held Mom tightly and cried for her and for myself. We were both afraid to speak of the outcome, so we just held each other, trying to gain strength from the embrace. She had to remove her teeth for surgery, something she hated to do, and suddenly she looked so old and frail. My dad was quiet, afraid to say what I was sure he was thinking. So many years, so much time wasted. Why do we spend our lives trying to achieve our goals but forgetting to enjoy life along the way? The bitter arguments and cross words seemed so senseless now in light of the possibilities.

Dad was restless. He was just anxious for all of it to be over. John and he were going downstairs to the cafeteria, but John opted instead to walk alongside Mom and me down to the surgery waiting area. We went to the recovery room to wait for the surgical nurses to come for our mother. The recovery room was deserted except for the nurse on duty whom I happened to know, as she was the mother of a friend I had met from my son's preschool days. Her son was in class with Todd for two years, and I had depended on her several times this past year to help care for Todd while my mom was in the hospital. I would send Todd to Brendan's, and Emily to Ellen's, and I felt blessed to have such good friends.

How strange it is when I stop and realize how the Lord has moved in my life, replacing old friendships with newer and better ones. He has brought me to my present church where I have been

IN THE PALM OF HIS HAND: MY JOURNEY OF FAITH

able to grow in my spiritual life. Emily was baptized here, and it was then that I found out that the pastor, Father Ted, was a longtime friend of both my mother and my grandmother. As a youth, he delivered newspapers to my grandma, and when he was to be ordained a priest, he sent her an invitation which she held on to all those years in a small metal box filled with mementos she felt were important enough to save. As a nurse, my mother had cared for his mother, possibly even at the time of her death.

I took all the mementos of Father Ted's that Grandma had saved and put them in a scrapbook which I gave to him after my grandmother had passed away.

My grandma's death was a beautiful and peaceful death. How I hoped and wished that my mother's could be the same.

"Just don't let her suffer, Lord," I prayed. I even went so far as to ask the Lord to take my mother this day if the outcome were to be cancer.

I couldn't bear the thought of her having to undergo extensive chemotherapy and radiation treatments. She was so weak. Her frail form had dropped to ninety-four or ninety-five pounds. The doctors were able to build her up a little bit. She even received a pint or two of blood the night before surgery, which upset her tremendously, but which her doctors felt was necessary for her to have.

When the surgeon walked into the recovery room, I introduced him to my brother. Since it was time to go into surgery, we kissed mom good-bye, and they wheeled her into the operating area. The surgeon said he would meet with us after surgery to discuss the outcome. It was 10:15 a.m. when we left to go downstairs. Surgery was slated to begin at 10:30, and since this was a gallbladder removal, I was prepared to wait at least a couple of hours. I met a friend from my childhood who was employed as a secretary, and joined her for some encouragement.

We had always had a pleasant friendship, perhaps because our birthdays were just a few days apart, and we thought along the same lines. Paulette had just lost her father to cancer last December, just before Christmas, so she knew how I was feeling at that moment and tried to give me a bit of hope. Paulette and I parted company, and I left the cafeteria to go by the chapel. I wanted to light a candle for my mom but was unable to find the votive candles, so I just knelt and prayed.

"Lord, please let my mom be okay," I prayed as the tears streamed down my face. I recited an Our Father and really meant the part that stated "Your will be done." I made the sign of the cross, genuflected, and left to rejoin my brother and father in the main lobby waiting room. I worried that the surgery might be too long, or worse, too short. I fought back the tears and set to work on my daughter's Bambi costume for Halloween. Emily modeled it for her grandma just last week at the hospital. My son made me promise that he could model his costume too when it was finished. Finish it? What if I never get it started? He had decided he wanted to be a dinosaur. The pattern was not an easy task for me to undertake since I was not an accomplished seamstress.

Funny though, the day my grandma died, I remembered that she had taught me how to sew, and I told her how thankful I was that she took time to teach me. She looked a bit puzzled when I told her that, but I was just expressing my thoughts out loud instead of holding them inside, and she did not have to understand. I can still remember the first thing I made with Grandma Kenney—a red cotton jumper. The pattern had darts that I, as a child of seven or eight, thought were interesting to do since I got to use the tracing wheel to outline them on the material. It fascinated me that these little white dotted lines magically appeared on the material. Grandma then showed me how to stitch those lines together, and I was amazed at the results. Grandma had so much patience.

IN THE PALM OF HIS HAND: MY JOURNEY OF FAITH

I was brought out of my reverie when the receptionist announced our name and said that Mom was out of surgery. It was only 11:15 a.m. "Too early," I thought to myself. I glanced back at the clock again, hoping it was later than I thought. It had only been an hour. The surgeon couldn't possibly have had enough time to remove her gallbladder, or could he? The thoughts raced through my mind as I gathered up my belongings to go upstairs to the surgical waiting room where we would get the report from the doctor. As we made our way to the elevator, my brother and dad made lighthearted conversation and seemed to be sure that the news would be good. I could feel my heart racing as thoughts ran through my mind. Too short. Did she die? Was it cancer? What did this mean? "Oh, Lord, be with us," I prayed.

The elevator ride was short. As we stepped out, I felt weak-kneed and scared. We went to the lounge and waited for the surgeon. There were a few other people there, and the television was on. Dad became an active participant in the game show that was airing at that time. My stomach was in knots. John paced nervously around the room. Then the surgeon appeared at the doorway to the lounge, and suddenly I wished we were alone in there with no outsiders around us. He sat down across the table from me. I searched his face for an encouraging sign, but there were none. How strange to think that this poor man whom we had just met a little over a week ago had to be the one to give us the news of our mother's condition.

He began slowly, saying that he wished the news were better, but grimly added that it was not. She had made it through the surgery, if you consider opening her abdomen, taking a small section out for analysis, and closing her back up, surgery. The analysis was definite. *Cancer.* The word echoed through my mind. How? Why? Why wasn't it discovered before? He said it was very extensive, a large tumor covering several organs and muscles. His prognosis? Six months at best, if she recovered from this ordeal well enough to go

41

home. The next forty-eight hours were critical. The tears streamed down my face. I couldn't bear it any longer.

My brother and I comforted each other and cried. I could feel my brother's strong arms about me and wished they could make this pain go away. My dad didn't cry then. Perhaps he couldn't right then and there. He waited until he was alone later with my brother and then broke down. I was glad he was able to cry. I know how hard it was for him, especially since he had lost so many people in his life whom he loved so much, and perhaps that was why he always appeared so gruff on the outside.

Thank God my brother John was here with us to help deal with this crisis. He called my brother Doug to tell him the news. I called my church, Mom's church, my good friend Pat, and tried to reach my husband. He didn't hear the phone, as he was asleep after working the midnight shift the night before. I was finally able to reach him by phone some time later. My aunt was summoned to the OR waiting room so that we could share the news with her. She worked as a volunteer and was at work that morning. I told her that it was cancer and sobbed on her shoulders. Why? Oh, why didn't she die? Why was God letting her live in this way? What value is it for her to suffer?

Friends came by, nurses who worked with my mom, offering their condolences. The recovery room nurse came by and gave me a hug and said that she was sorry about the news. She told us that Mom was in the recovery room and very alert. I looked at my brother and Dad, wiping away the tears, and asked them who was going to tell Mom. My dad turned away. This was another confrontation that he would rather not face. He had lost his mother and father at a very young age, making him an orphan as he entered his teenage years. He was never very good at expressing his feelings, keeping them mostly inside. I looked over to John and told him that since he was the oldest child, it was his job to break the news to Mom. I knew I just

IN THE PALM OF HIS HAND: MY JOURNEY OF FAITH

couldn't be the one to tell her. Dad and my brother left to go back up to Mom's room to talk to her.

I left the lounge to go for a walk and clear my head. I stopped by the office where my friend worked and shared the news with her. Paulette held me close and said how sorry she was. After I left her, I didn't remember where I went, but eventually I wound up back at Mom's room. John said that Mom took the news well.

I knew how hard it must have been for him. As a restaurant manager and area representative, he had to learn how to deal with employees and the public. He had to fire those employees who didn't pull their own weight. He hated that part of the job, but it was part of his job and his responsibility. Now, he had to be the one to break the news to our mother that she was going to die. I'm sure he wished that he could be back firing an undependable busboy or manager instead. I went into my mother's room alone and wept openly, cradling her hand in mine. I wondered how many times these hands had held a dying patient or comforted the families of the ones that were dying.

My mother's nursing career had spanned four decades. She had graduated from St. Joseph's Nursing School in 1933. She went to work at Little Company of Mary near Chicago. During that time, Mom met many acquaintances who became dear friends over the years with whom she remained in contact throughout her life. One of these people she met was a woman who over the years became one of her dearest friends. I recall the time Mom rode on a train with me to Louisiana to visit my friend Maggie. She went on to see her friend Edith in Lake Charles, then came back for me on the trip home. Mom and Edith enjoyed each other's company, they could share a good laugh together or just enjoy walking in the early evening together, talking about their dreams, enjoying the aroma of fresh lilacs in the air. Mom was single when they met, and she enjoyed her life then and had many good friends. She continued living near Little

Company of Mary Hospital until she married my dad, and then they moved down to Joliet. He left for the army shortly after they married. World War II separated them, as he went overseas for forty-two months, and Mom went to work at the arsenal plant in Joliet as a nurse. The separation proved very strenuous for her, so she chose to leave town for a while to collect her thoughts. She traveled out west to Seattle where she stayed with her uncle Joe on his houseboat. She found work at a local airplane factory as an industrial nurse. She was there for several months before being summoned home by her mother who was ill and required her presence for moral support.

Upon her return, Mom went to work at St. Joseph Hospital and remained in their employ until her health forced her to retire in 1972. Retirement did not sit well with my mom. When I look back over the years, I remember so many times that my mother was ill. The year that she retired, she almost died from a blood clot in her lung. She spent several days in the intensive care unit cared for by her fellow nurses. ICU was a very busy and hectic environment to work in. Mom had worked the third floor for many years at the old hospital, so when the new hospital was built, she was among the nurses chosen by Sister Therese, the hospital administrator, to head up the brand new ICU. Mom was honored to think that they thought her capable of handling such a responsibility at her age. After all, she was fifty-four years old at the time, many years older than her fellow nurses. She had to return to schooling to learn how to read the various monitors and learn new techniques. She did quite well, finishing at the upper percentile of her class. Although Mom was not a charge nurse, as she was never allowed to work the required hours for the job, she was "in charge," and became a mother figure to the many new nurses fresh out of nursing school. They affectionately called her Mother B, and thought of themselves as her "daughters." I knew that when her death occurred, I should have many "sisters" to weep with me.

The doctors saw her in a different light. To them she was Sarge, a title of respect and admiration. They knew she could not be bullied like many of the young nurses, but they also knew that they could depend upon her to carry out their orders precisely. So when her failing health forced her to retire, she met it with anger and resentment. Nursing was the first love of her life, one that did not want to leave her quietly for any reason. The transition to retired life was a difficult experience for her, one that took its toll on her for the first several years, but finally she emerged from her grieving, found purpose for her life, and joined many groups—such as Birthright, medical missions at her church—and became interested in life again. Her contributions to these groups were deeply appreciated by many people. She touched many lives with her generosity of herself, sometimes just by being there.

I cradled her hand in mine again, weeping sadly for her, praying that God would be merciful to his faithful servant.

Wednesday, October 12

Mom seemed a bit perkier today. Her lips were parched and dry, causing them to crack and peel, so I tried to keep them moist with the lip gloss. We were able to share a little conversation, but she was very drained from the effects of surgery. My brother arrived around noon, with the newspaper in hand. We exchanged greetings, and he proceeded to tell Mom a few lighthearted jokes to lift her spirits. She managed to smile as she drifted in and out of her sleepy state. The time with her seemed to go by quickly, as soon I realized that it was once again time for me to return home. I kissed her gently on her lips and promised to return the following day. My husband was off that day, so we said we could bring the children up to see her the next night. The suggestion of bringing the children to see her was met with some opposition by some, but my brother assured me that it would be a great morale booster for Mom to see the kids. After that I felt more assured. After all, this was their grandma, and they understood that she was sick and they had been wanting to see her for the past week.

On the way out of the hospital, I thought about a program that someone had told me about called Hospice. I was not sure what it was, or if Mom could qualify for it, but I felt it was worth looking

IN THE PALM OF HIS HAND: MY JOURNEY OF FAITH

into. My main goal was her comfort and a chance for her to get a grip on the situation before she was forced to go home if that time came. I stopped in the social services department of the hospital and inquired about the Hospice program. The woman in charge agreed to review Mom's case to see if she qualified. I felt hopeful after talking with her that the Hospice floor, called the Bethany Unit, would be beneficial for Mom. I called my brother when I returned home and asked him to discuss it with my mom and dad so that she could be prepared for the evaluation that would take place the following day.

As I drove home, I thought about the day's events. I had raced up to the hospital that morning not sure how Mom would be physically and was amazed at how strong she was. I had immediately phoned my sister-in-law Darlene so that she could have the opportunity to speak to Mom when she was alone. Darlene was very fond of Mom, feeling that she was very much a mother to her through the many difficult years that she was married to my brother Doug. After all, Mom was a grandmother to her two boys, so there was a bond there not easily broken by a divorce decree. My brother John had also informed me that day of Doug's arrival schedule for the weekend, and I was not anxious to be around for that confrontation. Doug is very intimidating to me, and I don't know when I will ever be ready to deal with him. Perhaps never.

I just don't know. He has hurt me deeply in many ways, some of which I don't care to discuss nor make public, but he used me in many deceitful ways, telling me many lies throughout his fourteen years of marriage, which made it difficult for me to choose where my loyalty belonged. But when the divorce became inevitable, I did not have to choose. I knew where I could find truth and feel comfortable with my conscience. My thoughts changed to the present as I arrived home to receive hugs and kisses from my children and feel the strong arms *of* my husband around me, welcoming me home for the night. It was good to be home once again, to gather strength up for tomorrow.

47

Thursday, October 13

The meeting with the social services department was scheduled for one o'clock. I delayed my arrival at the hospital so that I could take my daughter, Emily, to preschool. I felt as though months had slipped by and that I had not seen her teacher in years. Emily's teacher inquired about Mom, and I told her as best that I could about her condition. She offered her sympathy, and I accepted it gratefully. Emily kissed me good-bye, and I left to go to the hospital. Luckily, her daddy was home today to try and maintain some sort of normal atmosphere to this anything but normal period of our lives. I wondered if our lives would ever be normal again.

When I arrived at the hospital, I was pleased to see my mom more like herself. The effects of the anesthesia had worn off, and she was more responsive to our presence. I bent over and kissed her, stroking her forehead as a bit of reassurance for myself, and told her that I loved her. She smiled back at me and told me that she loved me too.

We were soon joined by my brother John and my dad who arrived just before the meeting was slated to begin. Two women from the social services came in carrying their notebooks and holding sev-

IN THE PALM OF HIS HAND: MY JOURNEY OF FAITH

eral forms for us to read over and fill out. Mom was quite alert and interested in the program and what it could mean to her. The woman in charge began the meeting by explaining just what hospice was all about. The main goal of the program was to provide death with dignity for those who chose to participate actively in their remaining care and wished to be allowed to make those choices that they felt were the right ones for them. A requirement for those who wished to enter this program was to have been diagnosed with a terminal illness, such as cancer, and given no more than six months to live. I felt a hard lump in my throat as I realized that Mom had all the required criteria. Six months. I thought about that and wondered whether she might live to see the full six months. Right then it was too much to consider, and I returned my thoughts to the present and realized that the meeting was just about over. We then went on a tour of the Bethany Unit, which was the name of the hospital wing for dying patients.

As we arrived on the eighth floor and rounded the corner to the Bethany Unit, I could sense a change in the hospital atmosphere.

Passing through the double doors, we entered a quiet zone complete with carpeting, a family room with comfortable seating, television, and phone. The decor was cheery, designed to uplift the family's spirit who happened to be there. The wall paper was much more like something you might have in your own home, and they stressed that. This was a room for the family to use. It was even mentioned that sometimes family members would stretch out on the couches for the night when their loved ones were really critical.

The staff members were very caring individuals, and the head nurse on days was a "sister" to me, as she was a "daughter" of Mother B's, my mom. Judy was looking forward to seeing Mom despite the reasons for her arrival to the unit. She assured all of us that Mother B would receive the best care possible.

The staff of the Bethany Unit were special people. Each of them—whether they were workers on the cleaning staff, nursing aides, or the nurses themselves—had asked to work on that floor. Those employees and the numerous volunteers involved had chosen to help those patients and their families to face death with a more positive attitude. Death itself is not an easy thought to deal with. I admired those people, wondering whether I would have what it took when the time of mom's death arrived, but I was relieved to know that they would be there with us every step of the way during Mom's hospital stay.

We returned to Mom's room and told her how wonderful the Bethany Unit would be for her. She smiled and seemed pleased. The social services representatives left, assuring us that they would move Mom in just as soon as they could. I proceeded to share with Mom how wonderful it was up there, with the cheery private rooms and the great staff. She was relieved and anxious to get up there so she could have time to collect her thoughts and deal with her diagnosis. I was relieved, thinking that if my mother were to die before ever being released, she was in a perfect spot, surrounded by people she knew from her nursing days. Hopefully, too, any visitors she received would feel more comfortable in that area, especially if they were a little nervous about being there in the first place.

I left Mom to go home for dinner with my family, just in case they had forgotten who I was. We ordered out fried chicken, but I couldn't even begin to force it down. My stomach was in knots, and eating was not going to solve my problem. I now knew why I had put on a few pounds this past year. The good Lord knew that I would need them in order to survive this ordeal. We finished our dinner, cleaned up the children, and dressed them up a bit to take them to see their grandma.

When we arrived at the hospital, the children were thrilled to see both Grandma and Grandpa and, even more so, Uncle John! Emily

IN THE PALM OF HIS HAND: MY JOURNEY OF FAITH

was full of questions for Uncle John about her cousin Stacie. She was not pleased that Stacie was not with him and was not satisfied with his excuse of her having to attend school back in Colorado. Todd amazed his uncle with his terrific reading ability, being that it was only the second month of the school year, and for a first grader, he read well above average. Not to be outdone, Emily displayed her puzzle-solving abilities, and needless to say, Uncle John was impressed! Mom smiled at all of this, just feeling grateful to be able to watch her grandchildren perform. It was as though their presence brought back a purpose for her to go on, no matter how difficult her days ahead might be.

We gathered up the family and headed for home at about 7:30 so that we could get the children home and in bed before very late. Todd and Emily gave out hugs and kisses to everybody, and Grandma relished hers the most. As Emily laid her head in my lap on the way home, I sat stroking her hair with my fingers, thinking over the week's events. I spoke to my husband and told him that I decided that we should go ahead with our plans to leave town for the weekend and visit his parents. I hoped Mom would understand that I needed to get away. After all, it was my birthday, and I was feeling every bit of my thirty-six years at this point. I felt that as well as Mom was doing, she would be around for some time. Even her doctors were amazed to see how well she had bounced back from the surgery. The Lord was giving us time, but it was up to us to use it wisely. Perhaps, with a break from this crisis, I could come back refreshed and with a positive outlook for the next phase of the Mom's condition which, as they told us, was subject to change at any time.

After we arrived home, I phoned John to discuss our plans. He assured me that Mom would understand. He was leaving on Saturday afternoon, and my brother Doug was to arrive Friday night. John was going to pick him up at the airport, so our last time together would be the next morning. I was relieved that I would get a chance to say good-bye to him in the morning. John knew I was avoiding a confrontation with Doug, but he also knew that the road ahead of us was not an easy one, and I would have to bear most of it alone. I needed this time to think of all the things I wanted my mother to know most, not just that I love her, but that she was my best friend, a friend I was not eager to lose.

Mom had always been there for me, no matter what. It was hard to imagine life without a person so special to me. After all, she believed in me. I was worth something very important to her. I am her daughter! She was there to patch me up when I skinned my knees, hold me in her arms when I was sick with measles, mumps, and chicken pox. She depended on me for support, too, and many times we shared private thoughts about our lives.

I recall our shopping trips, stopping for a bite to eat, usually at the five-and-ten-cent store. She let me voice my anger when I broke up with my high school sweetheart, knowing all the time she was relieved that I had finally come to my senses. I did not make her job of being my mother an easy one. I was always giving her reason to pray for me, whether I was living at home, working, or running off to Europe for two months during the summer of 1971. She trusted me. Many times, I was sure that I did not earn that trust, but it was there, given freely to me, and she felt I would always come to my senses sooner or later. I'm sure she was quite relieved when I finally did marry and settled down to a hopefully normal life. She was quite fond of my husband, Ernie, and felt that he was the greatest. I think it amazed her that he was so handy around the house. She always told me just how lucky I was that married such a wonderful person. Believe me, I knew that I was lucky. I also felt that my luck had a lot to do with Mom's constant prayers for my life.

Friday, October 14

Emily went to the hospital with me this morning. She was not at all uncomfortable with her grandmother's condition. She was just Grandma to her. Emily entertained her grandmother by talking about school, her new friends from her school, and various other topics. When you are three, many small things become important conversation topics to be shared with a special person like a grandma. Grandma listened attentively, smiling all the while. I'm sure thoughts about cancer, death, and dying just didn't enter her mind at this time.

Mom did tell me though that the people had been in earlier to admit her into the hospice program and that they would be moving her to a bed in the Bethany Unit as early as that afternoon to room 802. I was pleased that the matter had been moved along so quickly. I told Mom about my plans for the weekend, and she said she understood. I'm sure she wished that her family was not in such a state of mess, but she knew it would take time and a many prayers to change the way it was now.

My mind wandered back over the week's events, and I recalled being so afraid that Mom would die the day of surgery that I even went so far as trying to obtain the nurse's cap she had requested me to bury her with. Somehow during the last months our conversation led to a discussion about her death, and I asked her if there were any special instructions I should know about. She said that she wanted to be buried with a nurse's cap from St. Joseph's School of Nursing, not just any cap. When I asked her whom I could obtain one of these from, she assured me that at that time I was to seek out Sister Dolorita, who would get the cap for me, except that Sister Dolorita had boarded a plane bound for California the morning Mom had surgery.

"Terrific," I thought. "Now where do I find a hat?"

Fortunately, the nurse who was caring for Mom at the time of her surgery was able to obtain one for me. I was lucky too because they had changed the hats when the nursing school was accredited as a college and there were only a few remaining hats of the older style. I found out later, that because this hat was for my mother, they waived the usual eight-dollar fee for it. A small compensation for her many years of dedication to this hospital. It's ironic, I think, how much that hat meant to my mom. Nursing was her first love, and the hat was worn with pride. Nowadays, you have to look for a pin or something saying "RN" to be able to tell the nurses from the aides. The one-on-one care just isn't there anymore. The hospitals cut hours, pay, and compensation, thus leaving the nurses and staff with a bitter taste in their mouths. Dollars are spent lavishly in waiting room decor and cafeteria face lifts, while patient care is somewhat overlooked. I'm sure my mom is glad to be out of this modern nursing arena. She took pride in her work and in caring for the sick. Those days seem to have all but vanished.

Her nurse motioned to me from the hallway. She showed me the hat, and I thanked her politely. I took it in to show Mom, which I guess surprised the nurse, but as I said, Mom and I had talked about this, so she was not shocked at the mention of it all. I am so glad that Mom and I could talk about these things. I wanted her funeral to be

IN THE PALM OF HIS HAND: MY JOURNEY OF FAITH

beautiful when that time did come, and would make every effort to see that it was.

The nurses came in after lunch and told Mom that she would be moving soon, so I decided to wait around and see her new room before we left. We were pleased with everything, and her flowers looked just perfect in their new location. The flowers had been arriving steadily since Mom's surgery. The long list of visitors was steady, including her brother Jack and his wife, Nellie, who had been there twice since the surgery. She also received many phone calls, each a welcome boost to her morale. Her other brother, George, phoned several times from California. The family and friends were out in force to let her know that they cared about her and would be with her through it all. Classmates from her St. Francis Academy Class of 1929 came by to wish her well. Nurses who worked with her stopped in to say hi. Old friends stopped in to renew their friendships, all of which meant so very much to my mother. She felt loved.

Saturday, October 15

As I awoke from my slumber, I realized that it was the morning of my thirty-sixth birthday. I turned to my husband, and he gave me a gentle hug and a pleasant smile. Soon, our quiet moment alone was rocked with squeals of delight as our two bright-eyed children bounded up the stairs to our room. Our three-year-old daughter announced that it was "wake-up time" and we should get up right now. We both wrestled with each of the children as they gave us hugs and kisses. They wanted to get going down to see their other grandparents downstate in Mattoon. We decided that any quiet time together was going to have to be at another time, so we got up, dressed, and prepared to leave. We stopped for breakfast at McDonald's, but I was still not able to eat anything. I had not eaten or slept well since this whole ordeal began.

    I phoned the hospital before we left, and they assured me that Mom was fine. I gave them a phone number where they could reach me, just in case, and informed them that I would be back in town the next day. The ride down to Mattoon was filled with thoughts of what the following months would bring. I prayed my rosary, asking the Blessed Mother to watch over my mother and restore her health,

IN THE PALM OF HIS HAND: MY JOURNEY OF FAITH

if that was the will of the Lord. I kept thinking that there must be a reason for all of this to happen in our lives. I asked the Lord to give me courage and strength to face the days and weeks ahead. The tears streamed down my face as I wept quietly to myself, trying not to let the children see my tears. They hated it when their mother cried. Perhaps, they thought moms didn't have reasons to cry, but I knew they would learn all too soon that we do.

We arrived in Mattoon at precisely noon. Lunch was at noon at the French's. The children were so excited to see their grandparents. Todd said Grandpa French gave hard hugs, meaning he squeezed you good and hard. They were very fond of their grandparents, and the grandparents were fond of them, too. Our children were the youngest of all the grandchildren, so that made it even more special for them.

We exchanged small talk, and they inquired about my mom, saying how sorry they were about the prognosis. I guess it made everyone stop and realize that we were not indestructible, that we were each approaching a new phase in our lives. Perhaps they were entering their final phase, and at the age of thirty-six, I felt that I was entering into the middle-age chapter of my life, not sure whether I liked the idea or not. I felt as though I graduated into the older generation after my grandmother passed away. It was then that I saw my parents as old. I had never viewed my parents in that light. After all, they were just my parents, with no age attached, until now. I thought of how we might be entering a new phase of death in our families. I dismissed these thoughts. I didn't want to allow them to grow in my mind. I would be happy this day. It was my birthday, and I intended to put on a happy face and enjoy it as much as could.

Danielle arrived to see us and to go shopping with us for my birthday outfit. She was my husband's daughter, and we had always had a great relationship. We enjoyed each other's company, and always enjoyed shopping together. Danielle graduated last June from high school and got married, too. She was attending junior college and taking business courses. Her main interest was fashion. She had always had a great figure, and I had often thought she would make a great model. Her dream was to own her own shop, and I truly hope she realizes that dream someday. Her husband, Scott, held a steady job with good benefits, and he was also an aspiring musician with dreams of being famous someday. I hope they grow together through their dreams. Dreams—that is what life is all about. Without our dreams and goals, we tend to wander aimlessly, without purpose or direction.

We left for the mall. Danielle and I checked out all the new fashions for fall, and she pulled out a few outfits for my opinion. It was flattering to me to be able to wear the same size as my stepdaughter, especially since we never could until I lost fifty pounds. Before that period in my life, we couldn't shop the same stores, much less the same department. That weight loss changed me in many ways. I gained confidence and self-worth. Danielle was one of my biggest cheerleaders when I took off the weight. She always told me how great I looked and how proud she was of me. I feel as if she were my own daughter, not just a stepdaughter. I respect and love her as though she were my own, and I think she feels the same toward me.

We finally selected a nice outfit, and I didn't even look at the price tags, which was unusual for me because I normally never bought anything that was not on sale. I had decided not to worry about that today. It was a birthday gift from my husband, and we were going out to dinner next week with some friends from work, so he wanted to cheer me up with something nice to wear.

We returned to the house and waited for Scott to arrive to go out for pizza with us to celebrate. Emily was so excited about seeing Scott. He was one of her favorite people. We figured Scott must be an okay guy if Emily liked him because she had been very picky about whom she liked in her first three years of life. When she was about a year to two years old, Emily seemed to dislike my mother. I

IN THE PALM OF HIS HAND: MY JOURNEY OF FAITH

didn't know what was wrong, but she would not warm up to Mom very well. I felt that must have hurt my mother, but she never let it show. Mom would always say to leave her alone, and they would eventually make up to one another. I was so glad that her attitude eventually changed, and now she was definitely Grandma's girl.

When Scott arrived we left for dinner. I was a mother-in-law now, and it seemed funny. Danielle and Scott seemed to be very happy and levelheaded about married life. I'm not so sure that I would have been that way had I married that young. Our conversation was lighthearted and anything but serious. We did not talk much about Mom's condition, mainly because the children were with us, and we didn't want to talk gloom and doom to them this night. This was a night to forget, and celebrate. The tears were reserved for after hours when I was alone with my husband in our bed. There I could cry, and he would comfort, holding me in his strong arms that I have come to depend on so much over the last nine years of marriage. He was my beacon in a sea of confusion and despair.

Sunday, October 16

I woke up when Emily crawled into bed with us. She was hungry and wanted to go downstairs. When we got downstairs, Grandpa scooped her up in his arms and asked how his girl was doing this morning. "Fine" was her reply, and she sat down next to her grandpa for breakfast. I went in and showered and dressed for church while Emily entertained her grandpa. Grandpa Bill was quite thrilled to be the center of attention for Emily, and was soon joined by Todd and Grandma. I woke my husband long enough to tell him that I was leaving for church and what the children were doing downstairs. His parents were more than willing to take care of the children while I went to church, so Ernie just rolled over and went back to sleep for a while.

While I was at church, I found it difficult to concentrate on the liturgy and found myself crying off and on, with not a Kleenex to my name. The Catholic church in Mattoon was very pretty. The old-fashioned decor brought back memories of a different era in the life of the Church. I loved the paintings on the ceiling depicting several beautiful events in the lives of Christ and Mary, and the angels had such a beauty to them. Most churches now are all but bare, with only a few statues to remind us of our roots. It seems now that the

IN THE PALM OF HIS HAND: MY JOURNEY OF FAITH

Catholic churches are returning to some display of the beauty of the artworks that were all but erased through the late sixties and early seventies. Although Catholics are often accused of praying to the statues, it is a sad misunderstanding on the part of many non-Catholics. The statues are merely a representation, visual aids of sorts, to help us relate to our Lord and the Blessed Mother and the saints. We visit museums and look at statues of many famous people from history, and no one thinks that is wrong. Why shouldn't our churches display the saints and other religious figures? After all, our church is a museum in a sense. The great cathedrals in Europe draw record crowds who come to admire the beauty of the religious art from the stained glass windows to the beautiful statues and wood carvings.

I'll never forget how impressive it was to me when I toured Europe for two months during the summer of 1971. I visited Notre Dame Cathedral in Paris, many others throughout Germany, Austria, Switzerland, and especially St. Peter's in Rome, Italy. I felt proud of the beauty of these churches and proud of my religious heritage. I hoped we would once again see a revival of some of the beauty in our faith. I especially enjoyed seeing pictures of a smiling Christ, who seemed so full of life and love, not so serious and serene. Our faith should be more joyful. If it is not, I don't see how we can attract more people to join us.

My thoughts returned to the present, and I realized that Mass was almost over. I thought of how I must return home and face my mother's condition. Cancer. The sound of the word devastated my mind. I was numb from the thoughts of what would be. I was so grateful that we were able to get away this weekend, to pause and gather strength for the next phase of the illness. I thanked the good Lord for not letting my mother die on my birthday. I could not bear the thought of that happening. I asked the Lord to be with me throughout the ordeal, to never let me feel that He has abandoned me. The loss of my faith now would be a terrible price to pay, one that I didn't feel I could survive.

Monday, October 17

I talked with Mom this morning. She was in terrible pain.

I had planned to go up with Emily to see her, but changed my mind. I ushered Todd off to school on the bus and phoned Pat to see if Emily could come play with Ellen. She said, "Sure." I am grateful that I can depend on her.

When I arrived at the hospital, Mom was fairly coherent. The nurses had just given her some extra pain medication, and it was beginning to take effect. She looked so old to me now, much older than her seventy-eight years. I tried to fight back the tears. It was so hard to see her looking this way. My mind was so full of confusion. One minute I thought that she was dying, and the next time I thought she would make it through all right. God, how I wished someone could tell me what was going on inside of her. How much longer? Would it be enough time for us? What did this all mean? She was asleep, almost looking as though she were dead. I was glad the medication controlled her pain. I couldn't bear to see her in such pain. Once in a while I would see her face wince in pain. The tears spilled down my cheeks uncontrollably as a release from the tension that I felt inside.

IN THE PALM OF HIS HAND: MY JOURNEY OF FAITH

Before she drifted off to sleep, she managed to tell me that her sons' visit over the weekend was pleasant. She also told me that my brother Doug from California was upset that he did not get the chance to see me, as he left early this morning.

I told her I was sorry for her sake that her children were not close right now, but I was simply not ready to deal with this part of my life. She told how he wept for me, which I somehow doubted was sincere, but I didn't want to upset her by telling her that.

I told her that I loved him as my brother but could not condone what had taken place with the family he had deserted. Doug had refused to support, monetarily or emotionally, Darlene and Brian, his son, who was approaching those awkward teenage years of discovery and frustration. God, if only he could see what he was doing to his sons by alienating himself from them. Despite all the frustrations of a divorce, I believed the children involved deserved to be loved, treated with respect, and encouraged no matter how the spouses feel about each other. I told Mom that he knew my address and phone number—I did not know his. This seemed to satisfy her for the moment, and I was relieved.

One of Mom's friends appeared at the door. She introduced herself as Dot, and she came over to Mom's bedside. She was obviously quite shaken to see Mom in this way, so I asked her if she would like to step across the hall to the lounge where we could talk without Mom hearing us. She went on and on about Mom—telling me how great she was, what a wonderful woman my mother was—and she cried openly at the thought of losing such a good friend. I knew all of this in my heart, but it sure was nice to hear from people that my mother knew. My mother was involved with the cathedral seniors' club, and they helped make cancer pads for patients at home. "How ironic," I thought, in light of my mother's diagnosis. Life sometimes deals us a strange hand. As this woman spoke kindly of my mom, I thought to myself how strange it was for me to be consoling her,

63

rather than the one being consoled. I thought of my husband, who always told me that people find it easy to confide in me. He laughed at me when I spoke to strangers on the phone who called to purchase the diet products I sold, and within minutes they were pouring out their hearts out to me. I often had this same experience when I was out shopping and I met people in public. Perhaps, that was why I decided to join the Bereavement Ministry at my church, to utilize this talent God had given me to help those who needed someone to talk with or just listen to them express their grief. I even volunteered to be the committee chairperson. Funny thing, though I was not quite sure what I was supposed to do yet, I would keep trying and hoping for good results.

I can't help but wonder why there is so much unhappiness around us. It seems to me as though no one wants to take the time to listen to one another. We seem to think it is wrong to admit that we don't have all the answers. Somehow that makes us too aware of our vulnerability. There are so many hurting people in this world, and often the Church fails to reach out to these people at their darkest hour. I wonder myself how I'll be when my hour arrives. I guess I had already joined the ranks of the bereaved when my grandma died.

On the night Grandma died, I felt that I aged an entire generation. I faced her death with my eyes wide open, sitting at her bedside with my mother. I no longer feared death, and now I knew I would not be able to avoid it when my mother's time came.

My grandma and I shared a special relationship. Many happy memories come back to me, from sharing a warm glass of milk before bed—she was convinced it made you sleep better—to playing endless games of canasta and pinochle, of which she never seemed to tire. She taught me to sew, and although I was not a great seamstress, it was enabling me to make my children's Halloween costumes. I thanked Grandma for all the things that she taught me, and then told her that it was okay with me if she were ready to die. I could

IN THE PALM OF HIS HAND: MY JOURNEY OF FAITH

not hold on to her any longer as I had while I was growing up and beginning my marriage. I always had told her she couldn't die, but at the last moments before her death, a voice inside of me was saying that it was time to let go. I had been holding her hand most of the day, but then the voice said, "I can't take her until you let go." When I did, I bent over and kissed my grandmother good-bye and told her for the last time that I loved her. I went to my mother's side, and we exchanged some light conversation, and it was then that I noticed that Grandma had stopped breathing. I had known she was going to die. The moment I turned away from her and glanced out the window, the sun shone so brightly that it was as though the angels were coming to take Grandma to heaven. God bless her. I missed her and loved her so very much.

Dot left, and I stood watching my mother's breathing. It seemed so shallow and light. I hated to leave but knew I had to get home for my family. My father would not be coming in until around 5 p.m., and I hated for Mom to be alone. A lady appeared at the door. It was Mom's hospice volunteer, Ginny. She sensed my concern over Mom and offered to stay with her until Dad came up. I thanked her for her kindness and kissed Mom good-bye and left.

Tuesday, October 18

Mother snapped out of it again. The doctor had told us that there would be both good and bad days, so just when I thought that this may be it, she pulled through it again, surprising us all. I walked into her hospital room to find her sitting up on the chair, smiling at me. That beautiful smile again. It lifted up my spirit just to see it. Her doctors were amazed at her strength and stamina. Her surgeon came in soon after I arrived, and I asked him to go over once again exactly what his findings were during the surgery. He said the cancer was a massive tumor, extending everywhere from her diaphragm to her liver. I asked him how long she could have had this condition and why it was never detectable before this time. He answered me with a rather astonishing fact that she may have had this as long as ten or twenty years! That seemed so hard to imagine, but he said that it was a slow-growing cancer, one which was definitely in its final stages of development, and stressed once again that she probably only had at most about six months to live.

The truth was beginning to sink in: My mother was dying. She could be gone before Thanksgiving or before Christmas. The thought of not having Mom with us at Christmas was a thought I

IN THE PALM OF HIS HAND: MY JOURNEY OF FAITH

could not seem to bear at that time. Christmas was such a special time for our family. Ever since I was old enough to drive, I'd begun a tradition which had carried over to my own family with my husband and my children. I started going out to a local nursery to chop down our own Christmas tree. My dad was never too keen on the idea; the trees were either too tall or too wide. He did not enjoy all the fuss, but I never minded and went ahead with my plans anyway.

I really got into the Christmas spirit one year when I painted a complete nativity scene on their picture window. It turned out quite good, and admiration came from many of my parents' neighbors and several of my friends. I preserved that memory thanks to the Kodak film company. I even painted my bedroom windows with various Christmas scenes. I must have received a large set of tempera paints for my birthday that October because I sure went crazy painting windows that year. My dad finally insisted that I remove the painting from the picture window so that we could once again see out that window. Christmas had always been a special time for me; I always wished life could be as special as Christmas morning, with no hatred, no fighting, just peace. How I yearned for that peace right now in my life.

My visit with Mom was pleasant that day. We shared some special moments, talking about God and our faith, asking Him to be with us at this hour of our need. I pointed to the pin attached to the side of her bed. It was from Isaiah 49, which said that He will never forget us, that we were carved in the palms of His hands. She smiled at me and told me that I had been a great source of comfort to her. I only wished that I could wipe away this disease, this burden of pain and agony. I wondered why God allowed suffering. Surely there must be a reason for it. I stroked her hands, kissing them gently, and reminded her just how much I loved her. If only I could recapture more memories from my childhood to cherish them forever, but I knew that this was not possible. I was determined to concentrate on the time that we had left, no matter how long or short it might be.

Saturday, October 22

Mom was not well today. I kept thinking this could be it. The doctors told her the other day that because she was doing so well, that she could go home on Monday. I couldn't help but wonder if this had triggered her relapse, because she was not too keen on going home right then. I didn't think she was mentally prepared for what she would encounter after she got home. She was afraid of being a burden to everyone, of not being sure what she would be up against when she came home. I tried to gently reassure her that it would all work out. I kept telling her that I would be available three days a week when Emily was not in school to come and help her. She was so afraid of depriving my family of my time. I tried to convey to her that they would understand, but she didn't seem to want to hear that. Right there in her hospice room, the problems seemed miles away, with no questions to answer, just comfort and support. I wished that there was a way that I could change things for her, but it seemed as though we would have to try and live through this ordeal in some way. She was not going to pass quietly from this life as she would have probably liked to do.

IN THE PALM OF HIS HAND: MY JOURNEY OF FAITH

The doctors wanted her to take some radiation therapy to help control the pain and to try and shrink the size of the tumor. I wondered if this was advisable considering her weakened condition, but they kept insisting it would help, so Mom was willing to try. Her thoughts turned to what might happen as a result of this therapy, such as losing her hair. Her beautiful white hair. I always thought her hair was beautiful. As a child, I used to stand behind her on the kitchen chair and brush her hair, seemingly for hours. Mom always enjoyed that time of sharing between us. I saw it happening all over again with my daughter when she wanted to remove the rollers from my hair. She too enjoyed that time with her mom.

I smiled to myself at that thought, and Mom asked me what I was smiling about. I told her, and she smiled too at a time that now seemed so long ago for both of us. I assured her that we would buy the most beautiful white wig if it was necessary, but I prayed that God would not let that be necessary. I thought the embarrassment would be more than she could bear. I recalled seeing a former coworker, just a couple weeks before she died from brain cancer, who had a turban type hat on, obviously from the loss of her hair. I was sure that she too suffered from more than just the cancer itself, more from the vulnerability and inability to control what happened to her body from such treatments.

Mom drifted off to sleep again, and I thought about getting home to my family. Sometimes I wish there were no family depending on me at home, but I realized without them I would have no one to comfort me when I fell apart. With both of my brothers so far away, they could not help to shoulder all these terrible times and feelings of helplessness. My dad was having difficulty enough trying to handle himself without trying to comfort me. I wondered what would become of him when it was all over. I hoped and prayed that he would find a purpose for his life to continue on without my mother. I wondered, too, how I would handle myself without my mother there to talk to about thoughts I could not share with anyone but her. She was always interested in what I was up to, and always told me how proud she was. Or if she was upset, she would tell me. We had had such a close relationship, there were few secrets between us. She shared many confidences with me that perhaps she shouldn't have, but she and I trusted each other.

My sister-in-law Darlene always thought our relationship was unique, and she envied it to a degree. She laughed about the time my mother was upset with me over my mode of lifestyle at one time. Darlene said that even though she was mad at me, she still spoke of me with love and, of course, she always managed to laugh about it in the end.

A friend of Mom's came in, so I felt a little better about leaving her. She assured me that she would stay with her for a while until my dad came up after supper. She promised to call me if there were any changes that she felt I should know about.

I kissed Mom good-bye and left with a heavy heart. I hoped I could find a way to see her tomorrow.

Sunday, October 23

I was coming out of church, feeling a bit depressed, wishing there was some way I could go to see my mom without my children but not sure if I could find someone to care for them in my absence. The cost of finding babysitters was beginning to be a burden, but I still wanted to be with my mom to show her my support for her. I must have had a look on my face that expressed all of this, because a dear friend stopped me to inquire about my mother's condition. I told her that she did not look too well yesterday and that I wasn't sure if I wanted the children to see her that way. I explained that I was going home to find a sitter so I could see Mom. She would not hear of that and insisted that I bring them to her house for the afternoon. I started to refuse, but she kept on insisting, so I finally agreed. On the way to her house, I asked the children to be well behaved. They brought along their favorite toys, and after we arrived there, I discovered that they did not have to bring anything at all. Being a grandparent herself, her closet was well stocked with toys and games, so I knew Todd and Emily would be well taken care of. I kissed them both good-bye, and she told me to take my time.

When I walked into Mom's room, I discovered that my concern was unfounded. She was again sitting up in the chair, having her lunch. I must have had that look of surprise on my face because she said she was feeling more like herself today. I smiled and gave her a kiss on the cheek and hugged her shoulders. We had a really great visit, and she appeared to be optimistic about her state of health. What a relief! On the way home, it dawned on me that my mother was going to be around for a while, so I could relax and live a little once more. I prayed my rosary on the way home and offered it up for my mother, a sort of spiritual bouquet, similar to ones that often gave Mom when I was in Catholic grade school. We used to give them to our parents on special occasions, such as Christmas or Mother's Day and Father's Day. Now when I pray my rosary, I try to offer it up for a special intention or for a person who has a great need in their life. I have found much comfort in this, and almost always say a rosary on the way to town. It helps to calm me down and get my mind back in focus.

I arrived back at the sitter's to find two happy but restless children. I apologized for being so long, but she graciously excused it. I thanked her from the bottom of my heart, gathered up the children, and headed for home. It was such a relief to realize that Mom would be around for a while. I even managed to put a smile on my face when Ernie came home from work. He gave me a great hug and told me that he was glad Mom was feeling better.

Tuesday, October 25

I left Emily with Pat to play with her daughter Ellen while I went to the hospital to help my mother pack up her things and return home. Mom had been released, and she wanted me with her so I could help with the transition to home. I arrived early and found that Mom was downstairs for her therapy session. They were helping her regain some of the muscle strength she had lost since surgery. I decided to start packing without her since she wanted to be ready before my dad arrived to take her home. The room was bursting with flower arrangements that she had received in her short stay. Her friends and relatives had surely expressed their love and support in a beautiful way. Some of the fresh flowers had to be discarded, and many of them were beginning to show a fading beauty, but I knew Mom would want them with her at home.

She did not want Dad to pack up her belongings because she was afraid he would not take care to do it right. Sometimes I wished that they would quit picking on each other so much, but I supposed that it was how they expressed their love for each other.

To me, though, love just isn't supposed to be that way. When you love someone, you should uphold that person with the respect and caring that true love can demonstrate, especially for your children. Otherwise, they grow up with a distorted sense of love. I know that I did. I never knew what true love could be, and sometimes I wonder if I have truly learned it yet. I know that Jesus taught us how to love one another, but being human, it is not always so easy. I try and hope that through Ernie and our love for each other and our trust in each other, that my children will grow up confident and loving toward other people that they meet in their lives.

Mom and Dad, well, they just picked at each other. I suppose that it might be the perfectionist coming out in both of them. But whatever it was, being around them when they were picking at each other could drive a person crazy. I wonder what would become of my dad when he would no longer have this conflict to contend with in his life.

Mom has returned and looked tired but stronger somehow. The nursing assistant left her in my hands to help her to get dressed for the trip home. As I held her up, I realized how frail she really was, and I wondered if she would be able to handle things when she got home. I was so relieved to know that when she did go home, she would have an assistant come to help with her bathing and a nurse to monitor her medical needs. This was a great comfort to me because I could not be available at a moment's notice, and I would feel a bit uncomfortable helping Mom with her personal needs. Perhaps more than uncomfortable, I would feel clumsy not knowing how to help in many ways.

Lunch arrived, and Mom ate surprisingly well. As soon as Dad arrived, we loaded up the carts and ushered Mom out to the main lobby. The nurses and aides all stopped by to wish her well and told us to call at any time if there was a problem. When we got home, she decided to take a rest, so we settled her in to her own bed and hoped for the best. She seemed but just a little anxious to be home, so I tried to reassure her that the Lord would be watching over her and that

IN THE PALM OF HIS HAND: MY JOURNEY OF FAITH

she should not worry needlessly. We talked a little, and then I left for home after making sure that the needed medical supplies were there for her or were at least on their way. She needed a bedside commode so she wouldn't have to go down the hall during the night, and the visiting nurse made sure that one was ordered for her.

Late October

Mom made the adjustment to home quite well. Her stitches were healing nicely, and she was even talking about the upcoming radiation treatments with a positive note. She seemed stronger, but her frame had dwindled to about one hundred pounds. The Halloween holiday approached, and Todd and Emily were ready with their fifty-eight special costumes. I was amazed that I managed to finish both of them, especially the dinosaur, as it was very complicated for me and the pressure was on to complete it in time for Todd to model it for my mother in her hospital room. He was not about to be outdone by his sister who had visited Grandma in her Bambi costume just after her surgery. Grandma thought he made a great dinosaur, and so did the hospital staff. Now as the day arrived for the annual trick-or-treating, the children were ecstatic.

In the town where we live, trick-or-treat hours were always conducted on the Sunday before Halloween, so ours was to be on the thirtieth this year. Never mind the expense that this put on the residents of our town, as neighboring towns haul their kids in to take advantage of our off hours. We usually went through at least ten or twelve bags of candy which ran us about twenty-five dollars. The

IN THE PALM OF HIS HAND: MY JOURNEY OF FAITH

only positive side to this ritual was that the hours were during the daylight, so the small children were safer from any dangers that arose as the sun went down. There had been many times when my parents had to come down for the afternoon because my husband was working and I needed someone to hand out treats while I took the children around the neighborhood.

This year was different. We had our Sunday celebration, and my husband was there too. I decided to go up to my parents' house this year and make it just a bit more special. That way, Mom could see them all dressed up together. We took their picture, and they loved it. Mom's neighbors were tickled to see the kids in their costumes. I saw people whom I hadn't seen in several years, and many of them did not recognize me. Once I told them who I was, they inquired about Mom and how she was doing. I told them she was doing okay, and many of them said that they would try to come over to see her. I told them to be sure to call first, in case she was resting. The holiday was a huge success, and the best part was that Grandma was a part of our celebration. The days were growing shorter; time seemed to be slipping away much like the autumn season. Our eyes became focused on the upcoming feast of Thanksgiving with all the preparations and planning.

November

The key, I'd decided, was to keep busy. I'd plunged myself into many activities. I joined the church choir, and the regular Monday night practices had given me a lift and diverted my attention from the present. The upcoming Christmas celebration was going to be beautiful and would require many added practice nights. Thank God that I had good babysitters who were reliable. I'd always wanted to be a part of the choir at my church, but until the babysitting service was considered reliable, I was hesitant to join. I felt awkward at first, not knowing many of the people, but the choir director made the adjustment fairly easy. Once I got to know the group of dedicated men and women, I felt a part of a very special group in the church family. I had always enjoyed singing, and my family had also been involved in singing. My dad and brother John sang to me at my wedding, making that celebration even more special. John once sang in a nightclub, and I always thought he had a very good voice, but he chose not to pursue it professionally. Dad, however, went as far as to record a song, but he destroyed it when my brother kept crying every time he played the record at home. Who knows, maybe he was just trying to sing along.

I tried to keep Mom's spirits up. I called her sometimes two or three times daily, trying to encourage her, to keep a positive attitude about her illness. She was making small improvements, but her weight still declined as she suffered with nausea. I tried not to get discouraged over this. As our children crawled into bed for the night, we offered up their nightly prayers for their grandma, asking Jesus to be near her, to protect her, and to make her well. As I listened to them saying their prayers, I got goose bumps hearing those child-like prayers of innocence and trust. Emily sometimes wondered where Jesus was, and I try as best I could to explain about heaven.

I told her that He was present to us in our hearts, and when we did nice things for others, we were showing the love of Jesus through ourselves. Of course, she didn't really understand, but she listened, and to me that was what counted. Since Todd had attended CCD this year, he had learned many of the standard prayers we often took for granted. He liked to say the Our Father now instead of Now I Lay Me Down to Sleep. He was also learning about values and how each of us was important in God's eyes and how we must love everyone, not just our friends. I tried to be a good example for him, although I knew that there were many things in my life that could use improvement. I would keep trying, though, and hope that the values would grow up with my children.

The time we live in now is so full of mixed messages for the youth that I wonder if we will succeed in keeping our values alive, but that is why I attend church, so that I can keep my eyes focused on my faith and learn to apply it in my daily life. I usually start off my days in prayer, and I have learned to ask the Lord to guide me daily in my tasks that often seem overwhelming to me, to let me know that He cares about my simple problems, and the big ones too. Mom and I often discussed my problems together, and she had tried to help me, offering her advice without trying to impose her views too harshly. I now appreciated that quality in her and would try to avoid subjects that upset her, especially our family problems.

Thanksgiving Week

The holiday was approaching quickly. I'd decided to have roast chicken, as my children liked it better than turkey. Mom and Dad were planning to come down for dinner, providing that she was feeling up to it. Mom had not been feeling well, so our plans were up in the air. Each time she had a setback, I found myself panicky. Mom tried not to get discouraged. She reminded me that she was not angry over this illness; she was content that her life had been good. She had had much moral support from the two visits from her sons, and her brother George from California had been back to see her since her surgery. She was so thrilled at that.

    I wondered why it seemed to me that we were not always involved with our families except when a crisis arose. We seemed to have waited until the darkest hour approached before we let Mom know we were behind her. It seemed that we had always been too busy with our own lives to see the needs of others around us. I was glad that I was still in the area so that she was not alone. Her friends had been good, letting her know that they were praying for her each day. Prayer seemed to be our only weapon against this hidden enemy that ravaged through her body, depleting her strength and leaving

IN THE PALM OF HIS HAND: MY JOURNEY OF FAITH

her powerless. She tried not to get discouraged and kept her faith strong.

On the eve of Thanksgiving, Mom had to be admitted to the hospital. She was severely dehydrated and below one hundred pounds at that point. She had been nauseated all week, up most of the night retching and perspiring profusely. Her bodily fluids were being lost so rapidly, and her lack of appetite was not helping her to replenish her nutrients. My thoughts turned to the possibility that this could be it, but I tried to keep my mind on the positive. Dad had decided to come down for an early dinner on Thanksgiving, and we tried to keep the atmosphere of the meal somewhat normal. Todd and Emily were sad that Grandma was not with us, but we told them that they could visit her that afternoon. They decided to attend a movie with their dad while my dad and I went to the hospital for the afternoon. The day was a little gloomy and very windy. Mom's room was not very cheery.

I brought her a care package for dinner and told her that she could have it when she was feeling more like eating. I tried to be cheerful and kept the conversation light. A cousin of hers whose husband was also in the hospital stopped in to say hello. My aunt Mary came by and spent a good hour visiting, trying to cheer her up by telling her all the things that her family was up to. Mom always liked to hear about Aunt Mary's family. Mom and my grandmother were so proud of that family's accomplishments.

They both thought that the Kenney family was the greatest. Never mind the setbacks that might be encountered, Mom thought only of the best things that were happening. She was especially fond of Aunt Mary's family group because they were the members of her brother Jim's clan. Jim was very special to my mother. She almost felt like he was her son rather than her brother because he looked to her as a mother figure. When he died back in 1952, she grieved for him as a mother would. That was a tough year for Mom. She lost both her brother and her father within six months of each other. Jim died a month before I was born, so I'm sure my birth was not as joyful as she would have liked it to be. She did survive that period of her life, but I'm sure it left deep scars on her emotions.

It was getting very dark outside, and the room became very dreary. The only light was irritating to both Mom and her room-mate, so when the children arrived, I knew we could not stay very long. Todd and Emily gave their grandma a kiss and hug, but we could sense that they were uncomfortable. We didn't stay long, and I think Mom was glad, as she was very tired. She seemed to be feeling better, so I told her that we were going to drive down to Ernie's parents the next morning, but we would return that evening instead of staying overnight. She was sure that she'd be fine, so I told her that I would call before we left. By morning, she had improved and had even eaten some breakfast. I promised to call and let her know when we got home, and she told us to have a good visit.

Her stay this time was not as pleasant as the first time that she went to the Bethany Unit. The hospital had undergone some major changes, and the unit had to take on additional responsibilities and more patients. They no longer had the time to spend with these terminally ill patients to offer their assurances and to calm their fears. The rooms were mostly semiprivate, so there was less chance for families to talk openly about their worries. The lady in my mother's room had bladder cancer, and the suffering on her face was hard to bear. Her daughter stayed with her constantly, offering her sips of water and trying to comfort her in any way she could. I realized after seeing her that Mom looked surprisingly better so far. My prayers had turned into ones of thanksgiving for each day that we had Mom with us. I had not let go of her yet. I still clung to her, unable to give her up yet. I kept telling God that He could not have her yet. Christmas was less than a month away, and I was not willing to lose her before then.

December

The holidays were rapidly approaching with extra choir practices to attend, presents to buy and wrap, and so many other holiday preparations. The Sunday after Thanksgiving, we loaded up the family and went out for our annual Christmas tree hunt.

Mom was feeling better and had even returned home. The kids were so excited about getting a tree. This year we found one about ten feet tall, perfect for the area by our open staircase. I insisted that the tree get a bath before it came in, as last year it was so laden with dirt that I couldn't wait to get rid of it. So when we got it home, we hosed it down. This was going to be a special Christmas. We decided to purchase a new dining room set and spent some time shopping the various furniture stores to find the right one. It was an expensive set, but we had waited ten years before we decided to invest in one. It was beautiful, and we were hoping to have all the chairs in before our Christmas celebrations got under way.

On December 10, Mom and I attended another very special Mass in Lombard. Father Kelleher was to be there on a Saturday afternoon, so I told Mom that I would take here there. We were still hoping for a miracle but went there to focus our prayers on healings of our minds and hearts, not just physical healings. As we entered the hall to the church, Father Kelleher was walking through to go outside and meditate before the Mass. When Mom and I came down the hall with her in the wheelchair, he stopped us and spoke to Mom, asking her what her special needs were that day. Mom reminded him that she had seen him earlier in the year, how she truly felt that God had healed her then, and hoped He would see fit to touch her once again. He smiled at her and promised to pray especially for her during this celebration of the Mass.

The Mass was very special to Mom that day, as the friend with whom she had offered to share her healing with the last time was there with his wife. They too were seeking a miracle. The atmosphere was one of anticipation seeking God's intervention.

As I looked around, I saw needs so great, even greater than my mother's. I looked at the young children coming in with their wheelchairs, specially designed to accommodate the various needs of these special people. My heart went out to the parents of a severely handicapped young boy who was obviously quite retarded in addition to being in a wheelchair. I wondered how these people were able to cope, to keep going in spite of these handicaps. I wondered if I could handle such adversities. My children were blessed with good health and intelligent minds, and my problems seemed so meaningless in light of the suffering that these parents must be suffering. I made a mental note to be sure to thank our Lord this day for the tremendous blessings He had bestowed on my family despite the hardship that we now faced with my mother. "Oh Lord, that we might be conscious of our good fortune, less complaining and more appreciative," I thought to myself.

I turned to my mother, sitting beside me in her wheelchair. I had finally managed to unravel the knot in the chain of the necklace I had bought for her this past week. It was the child in the hand from Isaiah 49, the same one that I had given her in a pin form. I was at

IN THE PALM OF HIS HAND: MY JOURNEY OF FAITH

the Christian bookstore and saw this beautiful gold necklace of the symbol that had become our motto. I couldn't pass it by, so I brought it home, had it blessed, and brought it with us today. Just before the Mass was to begin, I put it around her neck and, as she smiled up at me, bent over her and gave her a hug. As I hugged her frail frame, I could feel the bones that seemed to have no muscle to them at all. As the tears welled up in my eyes, I quickly turned away so she would not see me cry.

The Mass was a comfort and seemed to calm me down inside. During the Our Father, Father Kelleher came out into the congregation to hold hands. Mom nudged me, and I noticed that he had taken the hand of her friend's husband who had cancer. She was thrilled and was eager to know his response to this healing service. After Mass they announced that the blessing would take place in a separate room, except for the people in wheelchairs, who would be blessed first in the church. Mom seemed anxious but eager to have the priests bless her once again. I stood next to her with my hand on her shoulder, letting her know we were in this together. Father Kelleher reappeared and moved directly over to Mom. He laid his hands on her head and prayed silently as the tears streamed down my face uncontrollably now. He kissed her on the head and told her not to give up, to keep on praying for her healing. He laid hands on me, and I felt so warm inside. I asked God to give me the strength I needed to deal with all of this—her illness, the possibility of her death, our family's needs for reconciliation, and the needs of the many people here today.

As we turned to leave, Mom seemed to be more content. Her smile lifted my spirits. We spoke to her friends on the way out, and they too were impressed by this service. We left to find the washrooms and then looked for the classrooms that were set up for extra prayers. Mom wanted to pray for her family and friends and felt that this would be the right time. We patiently waited for our turn outside in the hallway, and I glanced around at the many hopeful faces waiting there with us. As we sat waiting, a young boy struggling with crutches made his way down to the prayer room. I watched him as he painstakingly took each step, amazed at the determination he showed in his face. He smiled a bit and hurried in the classroom. He had some sort of monitor hooked up to him and a portable oxygen tank attached to his hip. I was intrigued by him, and when we finally came in the room for prayer, he was making his exit. I asked the woman who was our prayer leader what his problems were. She told me that just a few months ago at another service led by Father Kelleher, this same young boy who just walked out the door had to be brought in a wheelchair as he had no muscle strength at all. After that service, the boy experienced a miracle and was now able to walk on his own with crutches. He was a definite sign for all who saw him.

After the boy left, our prayer leader turned to us and asked us what our needs were that day. Mom began by asking for prayers for my sister-in law Darlene who had been struggling with MS. She explained that although she herself would like to be free of her cancer, she felt that she had lived a full life. She related prayers at my birth for God to allow her to live long enough to see me raised and out of the house. She told the prayer leader that God had given her all of that and much more. She stated how proud she was of me and how I had turned my life around, from one of self-destruction to one of which she felt proud. I turned away somewhat embarrassed to have my mother praising me so in front of these strangers. The lady smiled, saying that was wonderful and asked us to join hands in prayer.

As she offered up her petitions for us, she invited us to add our own petitions as our Lord was leading us to do so. I felt the need to pray for our family that we would once again be united in our love for each other despite all that had happened to separate us over the past years. I resolved in my mind to let go of the hurt I had felt at the

IN THE PALM OF HIS HAND: MY JOURNEY OF FAITH

hands of my abusive brother. I resolved not to let this injury grow into a larger-than-life hurt. I knew I had to get this feeling out but kept it inside, just between the Lord and me. He knew, and I knew He would help me overcome these feelings that sometimes left me feeling less than human. When we ended our prayers, my tears were flowing down my face like a river. They were tears of release from all these awful feelings that had been building up inside. I resolved to focus my attention on the present and let go of the past.

We left the church and headed for home. Mom was obviously quite tired out from all this excitement. We stopped for lunch and decided on tacos. It always struck me funny that Mom liked tacos, because she never ate anything like that before. She hated pizza and was not very fond of spaghetti, but she liked tacos. She had a friend—Marge, who worked with her at the hospital—who introduced her to this new food, and she surprisingly took to it quite well. Her friend had long since passed away, but the memory of her was instilled in Mom's heart, as are memories of many of her former friends and coworkers. As we sat eating our tacos, we talked over the events of the day and of the past month. The following week she would be going in for more radiation therapy sessions that were not designed to be a cure but simply to help with her pain control. They were very exhausting for Mom, so her days did not hold much interest for her. Dad took her in for her therapy and brought her home, where she collapsed into her bed for the rest of the afternoon. She thought they were helping somewhat, and she intended to finish the course of treatment that her doctors had set up for her. She was a very faithful patient.

I dropped her off at home. She thanked me for taking her and for the necklace, which she intended to wear every day, all day long. I was pleased that she liked it. I hugged her once again and kissed her good-bye. I felt better and hoped that she did too.

The weekend before Christmas, Danielle and her husband, Scott, came up to see her dad and me. They decided to come up while Scott was off so that they could have a Christmas celebration alone with us. They complimented us on the beautiful addition to our kitchen, the new dining room set, and said they were happy for us since they knew how desperately we needed it. Since Ernie had to work, I suggested that we go up and see my mom, as she was not able to come down. They agreed to go, and I promised that we would not stay too long, as I could sense their discomfort with the situation. Mom was thrilled to see them both, and we showed her their new dishes that she had picked out for Christmas from us. Mom was glad that they came to see her.

Mom had held a special spot in her heart for my stepdaughter and accepted her as her grandchild without any hesitation. She and Dad always remembered her on her birthday and on the various holidays throughout the year. I had been grateful too that Danielle had responded so well to my mother and father. I felt that she truly belonged as a part of our family. I had known her since she was four, and I used to babysit for her when her dad's shift schedule kept him from caring for her himself. I admired him for the way he took on the responsibility of being a weekend dad. He had been a good dad then and was probably one of the best dads now to our two children. Danielle allowed us to practice on her, and despite the many pitfalls of a divorced family, I felt that Ernie did the best he could, and the results are obvious. Danielle and Scott had formed a good relationship with us, and I felt that they were pleased with the acceptance that they had gained from all of us.

We stayed for about an hour or so, and then we decided to get going. Mom asked me to do a bit of shopping for her, especially the items she wanted to buy for my kids. I assured her that I would take care of it for her, and she seemed content with that. As we said our good-byes, I wondered if this would be the last time that Mom would

IN THE PALM OF HIS HAND: MY JOURNEY OF FAITH

see Danielle and Scott. I dismissed that thought and held on tightly to my prayer that Mom would be with us through the holidays. I told Mom to conserve her energy so that she could come down for afternoon dinner on Christmas Eve. We decided on that time because it would be easier for Mom and Dad. I was looking forward to that night also, as Ernie had agreed to accompany me to the Midnight Mass at our church to hear the results of the hours of practice that the choir had put in over the last month. My anticipation was building up to that night, and I was really excited.

The week was hectic, and I talked to Mom each day on the phone to check on her progress. She was tired but looking forward to our dinner. Mom and Dad arrived early, and we decided to open the children's gifts that their grandparents brought for them. The squeals of delight were reward enough. Their faces lit up as they discovered that they were the proud owners of new scooters. They couldn't wait to ride them on the driveway. We took group photos of everyone that day—the children and my parents—a photo of Mom and I, and everything I could think of because I knew in my heart that there would not be another Christmas to record with my mom, and I wanted memories to look back on in the future. Mom looked especially lovely in her tan suit that day. She always enjoyed wearing pretty clothes. As I held my arm across her shoulder for our photo together, I could feel her bones protruding, indicating the immense body tissue loss that had taken place over the year. She smiled that tight little smile of hers as if there was no trouble at all, but we all knew better. This was to be our last Christmas together, and all of us were painfully aware of that fact.

We all gathered around the new dining room set for a lovely Christmas meal. Mom and Dad were so proud of our new acquisition, which by now included the remaining four chairs. Mom had always wanted so many things in their house which she very seldom acquired. It was such a shame to think that they lived all their lives never satisfying their wants or desires, always wishing upon a star but never having those dreams fulfilled. I remember once that my mom wanted an expandable table for the living room so that when they had a party, they would have a table large enough to accommodate everyone. But, alas, the dream remained just that. When I purchased a used table like that for our kitchen to help out at party times and holidays, she was glad that I had at least fulfilled her desire in my life. The new hutch that Ernie and I bought was large enough to show off Mom's many fine crystal and china pieces that have been handed down from her mother to me.

My favorite pieces were the knife and fork rests made out of cut glass. They were my favorites from my youth, too. As a young girl, I used to love when Mom would let me set the table with the best china and silver for the special holiday dinners. I would adorn the table with a tablecloth and candles in the special cut-glass candleholders and the special dishes or Bavarian china, white with a gold rim around them. She had enough for twelve or more place settings, complete with demitasse cups which, of course, were seldom used. The china came from my mother's uncle who was engaged to a girl from England. Before the marriage took place, a problem arose, and the wedding was called off. She left her dowry, which included the silver and china and other items. Somehow they came into my grandmother's possession, and she eventually passed them onto my mother, who told me that they would someday belong to me. Mom would enjoy these special times, and perhaps that was why I always enjoyed the fuss and muss at holiday time.

My biggest problem at times like these was remembering to put the rolls in the oven, but I managed to get dinner on the table without too much trouble. Before we began our celebration, we lit the candles on the Advent wreath and read the Scripture passage for the day, reflecting on our lives in the last year and asking for God's guidance and encouragement for the coming year. I thanked God

IN THE PALM OF HIS HAND: MY JOURNEY OF FAITH

that we were all together that day, and the tears welled up in my eyes. So I tried not to talk long; otherwise I knew I would lose control. At the end of our prayers, everyone said, "Amen," and I smiled, thinking how precious my children sounded when they prayed.

I hope that my children become more confident in their prayers as they grow up. I hope that they never feel separated from God and that they know He listens to us when we are in need and when we are not. Of course, we may not always listen to Him when He tries to direct our paths.

The afternoon hours rapidly slipped away, and evening approached. Mom was quite tired. Dad suggested that they return home before it got dark outside, and Mom reluctantly agreed.

They thanked us for the lovely dinner, got hugs and kisses from our children, and turned to leave. I gave her a hug and told her how much I loved her. She smiled and told me she loved me, too. As they backed out of my driveway, I paused to think of how old they had suddenly become to me. Although my parents were always older than most of my friends' parents, I had never regarded them as old until now. It was a hard fact to deal with because it meant that I, too, was getting older, and I might be forced to grow up whether I want to or not.

I quickly dismissed those thoughts and turned to the evening's plans that I had to arrange. The children had to be bathed and read to and tucked in their beds before my husband and I could leave to go to church for Midnight Mass. The children were very excited about Santa's pending arrival, and the anticipation of what would be under the Christmas tree in the morning filled them to the brink of hyperactivity for the evening. It was quite a job to settle them down and get them to sleep. Todd assumed his sleeping quarters at the top of the stairs, an old cot that he liked to use when we had company staying with us. He slept there hoping to catch Santa in the act as he placed their presents beneath the tree. The neighbor boy came over to stay with the children while we were at church. He told us later that Todd had awakened and saw the presents under the tree but went back to sleep after he called out his name. Thank goodness, or we might have missed the unwrapping of all the gifts while we were at church.

The Midnight Mass was beautiful, and the choir sounded great. There were many extra musicians with their instruments, a very talented soloist, and many other special effects. As communion time approached, my eyes focused on the Lord hanging from the cross. Our cross reflected the risen Lord, with Jesus fully robed and His hands outstretched up to heaven. He seemed to be telling me to let my mother go, that He would take her and care for her from now on. As much as hated to let go, I knew I had to for her sake. As we prayed the Our Father, I tried to concentrate on the prayer and sincerely mean the words that I was praying. I lifted my eyes back up to the cross as I prayed the words, "Thy will be done," and offered my mom up right there, saying that she was His to do with as He saw fit. I could hold on to her no longer. I asked for His mercy and hoped He would not allow her to surfer needlessly. I asked, too, for the strength that I would need to endure to go through our remaining time in a way pleasing to Him. As we said "Amen," I thought, "So be it according to Thy will, not mine."

Monday, January 16

I had decided to keep a daily log on my mother, her condition, her progress, my emotions, and the effect that they had on our lives. I was going to keep two records, one where I would reflect back on last spring, trying to recapture events, feelings surrounding these events, and record them as best that can so that when my mother does die, I would have a permanent journal depicting our lives and how this illness had affected us. I wanted something recorded so that my children and the rest of our family would be able to pause and reflect on this phase of our life cycle. I wanted a memorial for my mother so that my children would know that Grandma loved them very much, how she loved them to give them reminders of their moments with my mother. From here on I would keep a record of our days' events, with the hope of showing how we were progressing toward her impending death.

  Today was a school holiday honoring Martin Luther King, and so we decided to visit my parents and run a few errands in town. We purchased a "new" used car the other day, a taupe-colored '85 Cadillac Seville, and my husband wanted to have the oil changed. It was a beauty. This was the third Caddy that we had owned, but it was by far the best one we had ever bought. I hoped to keep it a long time. While my husband was out having that errand taken care of, Todd and Emily and I visited Mom. Emily was not in a very pleasant mood and would not make up to Mom at first, but she eventually settled down. I sat across from Mom on her bed and was helping her sort through her Christmas cards. She was overwhelmed at the immense task of sorting. I tried to assure her that it didn't matter, we would get through this one way or the other. I tried to convince her not to worry, but I don't know how or if I could handle all this responsibility.

I had been trying to find one of Mom's old nurses' caps but was not having any luck. I asked my best friend, Donna, if I could borrow one of hers to use at the presentation of gifts during the liturgy at the time of my mother's funeral. I thought of this idea after I read the book *Through Death to Life* by Rev. Joseph M. Champlin, which was designed to give families the opportunity to actively participate in the loved ones' funeral liturgy as a way to work through part of their grief. I had already picked out the songs and readings that I would like to use. It was something I felt I should do, taking the idea from not only the book that I read but also from a video entitled *Life through Death: Working Through the Pain of Grief* by Ken Czillinger, a video dealing with grief and its cycles.

We had been showing this video in stages through the bereavement ministry at our church. I felt as if I was planning a wedding, but on a more somber note. I hoped it would be beautiful. I had picked out several beautiful songs, most of them my favorites. I wished I could come to terms and tell Mom about it, but now just didn't seem like the right time. Perhaps I wouldn't ever be able to tell her.

Mom asked me to weigh her to see just how much weight she had lost this week. Fully clothed, including her slippers, she weighed a mere ninety-two pounds. She was so thin. As we talked, I remarked to her, "Mom, what am I going to do with you?"

IN THE PALM OF HIS HAND: MY JOURNEY OF FAITH

She turned to me with her hand on the kitchen counter and replied, "Just let me go."

I tried not to cry and told her that I had already given her up to God. I couldn't bear to see her suffer needlessly. I couldn't bear to see the pain in her eyes. My heart ached at her misery.

"Oh, God, why must she continue to suffer?" I asked in desperation.

Mom had noticed that people seemed to be avoiding her. She realized that they might be having difficulty handling her illness, but she needed to be comforted by the friends she had always depended upon to keep her going. I could sense the deep hurt that she was suffering. She was so depressed, and I couldn't seem to find the avenue to help her out of this depression. Normally, she would get out and find something to do to relieve the stress and depression, but now she felt trapped by these circumstances and her inability to escape from all of it.

By this time my husband had returned from his errands and took this as an opportunity for me to escape the present stress and run some errands of my own. As I walked out to the car, a friend of Mom's drove up. We exchanged greetings, and I told her how depressed Mom was today. She said that she understood, as she had been through this type of illness with a family member who died of bladder cancer. She said she would try her best to cheer Mom up, and so I thanked her and left. As I was driving to the store, I talked with our Lord, asking him to take her in peace soon, to end this suffering.

Wednesday, January 18

Mom called to say that she and Dad were coming down for the afternoon to visit. Mom said she'd be okay, that she would bring her morphine tablets along as a precautionary measure. Dad had run out to the store for a few things that I had asked him to pick up for me, and he insisted on bringing them down today. Mom said she didn't mind, that the change of scenery would help her feel a bit better.

When they arrived at our house, I went out to help her in. She looked so frail. Her walk had turned into a shuffle. She had to sit down as soon as she came in. We sat down in the kitchen and talked about general topics—the weather, fashions, anything but how she was feeling at the moment. Grandpa was out in the living room with his Emily. She sure did love her grandpa. It was so nice to hear them laughing and playing with each other. How I wished that I had had that type of relationship with my dad. We had such a volatile relationship, fighting constantly from about age ten to adulthood. We never exchanged conversation like normal family. We always saw opposite sides to everything until Todd came along. That seemed to change things because my dad would actually try to talk to me. I supposed I was as much to blame as he was for the lack of communi-

IN THE PALM OF HIS HAND: MY JOURNEY OF FAITH

cation between us. We just never learned to reach out in love to one another, and although we had made some progress, I doubt that we would ever have the ability to be totally honest with each other. That would take commitment from both of us, and I thought we were too afraid to trust each other completely. Despite this, thankfully, Dad was totally devoted to Emily and Todd, even more to Emily, because I think he thought that this was his second chance at having his "little girl."

Mom seemed to be a bit uncomfortable, but she tolerated the pain. She and Dad decided to stick around until Todd got home from school. Mom and I sat browsing through the new spring catalogs, checking out the new spring fashions. She pointed to the styles that she liked best, but then in exasperation, she exclaimed, "Oh, what's the use!"

She felt that she had no right to look ahead or to make any plans for the future. She had given up and felt ready to die. She didn't want to go on in this capacity. She was at peace with God, ready for Him to take her away from all of this. She was tired. I don't blame her. I asked her if she would like to attend a charismatic Mass this weekend at her church. She said she didn't feel up to it, but she said that she would think about it and let me know that day. In the meantime, I kept praying for her release from this suffering.

After they saw Todd for a few minutes, they decided to leave for home. I gave her a hug, and so did the kids. She looked so old to me now.

Thursday, January 19

Not much new with Mom. I went out to lunch with a friend. We discussed religion. She was having some doubts about her faith and whether or not the Catholic Church was meeting the needs of her and her family. I tried to encourage her with my support. I decided that I should invite her to attend the Mass at the cathedral this Saturday, which she seemed very excited about. I was excited too because I was hoping it would give me some relief from this stressful situation. I thought that it would prove inspiring, and I hoped Mom would decide to go.

Ernie left us for the weekend to go snowmobiling with a buddy. He planned to return on Sunday, and although I missed him terribly when he was gone, I realized that he needed to get away once in a while to blow off some steam. I tried to keep a positive outlook on the idea so that the kids and I would be able to survive these few days. How I wished we could go together, but I realized it was just too hard for us to go anymore since the birth of our children. We would, I hoped, be able to enjoy these activities once again when they were grown a bit, but by then we might have decided that it was not for us anymore. Who knows?

Saturday, January 21

We arrived at Mom's around 11:30 a.m. after having a great breakfast with the family at Bob Evans restaurant in Joliet. We were celebrating the fact that my husband came home early from his snowmobile trip to Wisconsin. His buddy's snowmobile engine had blown up, which put the end to their run time. Our celebration quickly ceased as I walked into Mom's room to find her disorientated, shaky, and burning up with a fever. I took her temperature which registered between 101 and 102 degrees. I called to my husband, who was an EMT, to come in and stay with Mom while I tried to reach her doctor. Ernie came in and checked her pulse and said it was a bit rapid. I reached the doctor's office only to learn that her doctor was not on call for the weekend. They suggested that we contact Mom's home health agency and have one of their nurses come out and evaluate her.

When I reached them, they seemed a bit reluctant to come out for just a temperature. I told them that I needed someone to come out and at least evaluate her so that I could decide what measures we should take for her care. They finally agreed to call out a nurse who was in the area and that she would get back to me to let me know when she could come to the house. As I hung up the phone, I could sense that Mom was slipping into a state of confusion, and I tried to comfort her as best as I could. I sat down on the bed and pulled Mom over to my shoulder, wrapping the comforter around her to try to warm her up. The nurse called to say that she would not be out until 1:15 or 1:30 p.m. It was noon now, so I sat back on the bed as best that I could and just held my mother in my arms.

Dad walked by the room and was shocked to see her so ill. She was fine this morning. She even had her hair washed and set by her friend Marce. He tried to get me to let her lie down alone, but I told him that I was going to hold her and try to comfort her in my own way. He walked away, probably wishing that he could provide some kind of comfort to her but not knowing how to do it. She lay with her head resting on my shoulder for over an hour, not responding or saying anything. It was almost as though she was asleep or unconscious. While I was holding her, my eyes fell on a picture of the Sacred Heart of Jesus, whose outstretched arms seemed to reach right out at me, and I extended my arms in an outstretched manner toward the picture, as though to offer up my mother to Him. Thoughts raced through my mind, and I couldn't help but wonder if she would die right then and there in my arms. Finally she seemed to want to lie down, so I slid out from under her, and let her lie on the pillows. I went out to refresh myself and wait for the nurse to arrive.

When the doorbell rang, both my children reacted with excitement. While I was in with their grandma, they had kept busy in the living room playing with Dad and Grandpa but occasionally peeked in on Grandma, trying to comprehend what was happening in her room. The nurse came in, and we took her in to see Mom. She checked her vital signs and tried to get a response from Mom, but she was incoherent. She came out to the living room and talked to all of us, advising us that she felt that perhaps this was the beginning of the end. She said her heart rate was very high and her breathing was very irregular. She thought perhaps Mom was going into kidney or

IN THE PALM OF HIS HAND: MY JOURNEY OF FAITH

heart failure. We had a choice to make—to try to weather this out at home, dealing with her death on our own, or to take her to the hospital—but she warned that the hospital would take more aggressive treatment and possibly prolong her death even longer.

The thought of keeping her at home scared the daylights out of both my dad and me, as I didn't think either of us was prepared to ride out this storm without the professionals to help us out. We opted for the hospital, and I could see the sense of relief in my dad's eyes. While we discussed our plans, the nurse called for an ambulance to transport her to the hospital. She also contacted the hospital, and we were told that there was an opening in the Bethany Unit, so Mom would be a direct admission to that floor.

When the ambulance arrived, Todd and Emily were quite excited and wanted to ride in the ambulance with Grandma, but it was not allowed. So after they got Mom on the stretcher, both of our children came over to Mom and gave her a kiss and a hug, telling her that they loved her. By this time, Mom seemed to snap out of her state of confusion and was pretty alert. She didn't remember anything until when the nurse had gone back into her room and told her that she was going to be admitted to the hospital. She was relieved but at the same time a bit afraid because I think she sensed that this could be her last trip there. All of us stood by as the attendants wheeled Mom out to the ambulance, telling her we loved her. I wondered if this was the last time my children would see their grandmother alive. I could sense their distress and wished that I could do something to change it for them. My husband drove me to the hospital. Dad was to follow up in his car. I arrived on the eighth floor right behind Mom. She seemed better than when she was at home, and I wondered if we had really made the right choice in bringing her in. They settled Mom in a bed, but the roommate smoked, which bothered Mom, so I asked that she be moved to a different room as soon as one became available. A short time later they moved Mom down to another room, and she seemed a bit relieved.

When supper arrived, Mom had only her dietary supplement, some pudding, and water. She was receiving some nourishment intravenously and an antibiotic to ward off any secondary infections. She seemed to slip down further right before my eyes. Her bladder was not functioning well, and her bowels were also not in proper order. She was so miserable, and I had to fight back the tears that just seemed to want to rush down my face. Mom must have sensed my emotions as I sat by her bedside stroking her hair and holding her hand in mine.

"I wish I could do something for you, Mom," I said a bit hesitantly.

She looked straight at me and replied, "You've done more for me than I could have asked for." Then she stated, "I hope this is it."

Choking back the tears, I replied, "For your sake, I hope this is it, too."

Mom proceeded to tell me how proud she was of me for turning my life around and becoming the person I am. I wished we could talk more in depth, but my dad kept interrupting, saying that he wanted to take me home. I didn't want to leave, not just yet. I wished he would just leave me alone, but he was persistent in wanting to get me home to my family. I tried to put him off and finally decided that I would leave after they put a catheter in Mom so that she would not have to worry about dirtying the bed again. I guess her bladder was not functioning as it should, because she could not control herself and ended up soiling her bed. This was a great distress to both Mom and Dad. I was sure that the embarrassment alone was hard to handle, let alone the inability to control or change the situation.

I stalled my dad as long as I could. I made phone calls. I called the church to let her dear friend Sister Lorraine know that she was in again. I contacted some friends of mine that did printing and asked

IN THE PALM OF HIS HAND: MY JOURNEY OF FAITH

them if I could drop by one day to show them the funeral liturgy and discuss how I wanted it printed. I sat in the lounge room and cried. I asked our Lord to take her or cure her, but I was tired of this emotional roller-coaster ride that I had been on since the beginning of this illness. I couldn't imagine living without Mom, yet I could no longer bear her suffering and pain. I tried to compose myself and went back to her room, where the nurse had just come in to insert the catheter for her. After the nurse finished, I went in and decided I'd better get home since my dad was still persistent that I go. Mom told me not to worry—she was not afraid to be alone. After she said that, I felt more at ease and decided to allow my father to drive me home.

When I got there, Ernie was surprised to see me, but he held me in his arms. That made me feel so much safer. I showered, then took a moment to write an entry in my journal before phoning my sister-in-law Kathy to talk about plans. I wanted to call Darlene also, but it was so late. I was tired and needed sleep.

Sunday, January 22

I got up and dressed for church. I stopped to talk to Father Ted and Sister Mary Pat before Mass to let them know that Mom was in the hospital, probably, I hoped, for the last time. I asked that they say a prayer for her peaceful death. We hugged each other; then I left to join the choir at church. I was there in body, but my spirit was with Mom at the hospital. I couldn't concentrate on the Mass or on the homily, as my thoughts were racing through my mind. I was anxious to leave so that I could get up to the hospital.

I stopped by my friends Don and Marge before I went to the hospital, to show them what I needed to have printed for Mom's funeral. They said that they would get it all typeset form and get a proof made so I could check for spelling and other errors. I thanked them for allowing me to come to their home on a Sunday. They were so nice, offering to let me stay the night if I found it necessary while Mom was hospitalized. It amazed me how some people could be so generous when they saw a need. These people were just casual acquaintances. I worked with Don many years ago, just after my high school graduation, and only recently got to know his wife, Marge, when they began a printing business in their home. When I

IN THE PALM OF HIS HAND: MY JOURNEY OF FAITH

went into business for myself, I decided to have them do some printing for me and had always been grateful for the friendship that they bestowed upon me so easily without hesitating.

So often in this world today, people are not eager to open up to others, to really be a friend to one another, yet these two were not at all afraid. I remember how much I admired the husband when I was younger. Don was like a big brother to me when we worked together. He always listened to my problems and never made me feel like I was imposing when perhaps I truly was. His wife was like him and had been a great comfort to me. One day shortly after mom was first diagnosed with her cancer, I ran into her in a local catalog store. She asked how I was, but I couldn't say anything and just cried on her shoulder over Mom's cancer. They had my admiration and respect for their understanding and their commitment to each other.

We chatted a bit about their remodeling project and their new grandson. Of course, a few jokes were thrown in as well which made me laugh, and that felt very good. We went over the material that I wanted printed, and then I thanked them and left to visit Mom, promising to call and confirm the color of the paper and any other additional ideas I might come up with. But as of that time I thought it was pretty complete.

I arrived at the hospital to find Mom improved a bit but still lying in bed. Her spirits were pretty good though, and again I became thrown off guard. She was a tough cookie; that's for sure. Dad came in and visited for a while. Sister Lorraine stopped in, and we all had a good time talking and sharing about our faith and strength in the Lord. She led us in prayer for Mom, asking the Lord to be with us and to reveal His will for Mom. As she got ready to leave, I gave her a rough draft of Mom's funeral liturgy, asked her to look it over and also to give a copy to the priests. I told her that I would have several of the final copies available for the staff at the cathedral when the time came, and who knows, maybe this was not the time. She was full of admiration for what I had done for my mother, but I was not doing this for the admiration. It was my way of dealing with her death and an expression of my love for her, a final tribute to her.

Marge, one of Mom's former classmates from Saint Francis Academy, came by to see her. They had a nice visit. While she was with Mom, I walked down the hall to the lounge and tried to reach Mom's hospice volunteer, but she was apparently out for the day. I was torn as to whether I should stay with Mom overnight or go home. The evening shift came on, and the nurse was very attentive to Mom's needs. They informed me that they would be doing a CAT scan tomorrow to see if there was anything they could do surgically to ease the pain from the incision from last October which had never healed properly. The pressure would build up so that eventually it would pop open and begin draining. Until it did, though, it caused her severe abdominal pain. I wondered how she could tolerate this pain so well.

Aunt Mary came by to see Mom, who was pleased to see her. At least while she was in the hospital, she would get a number of visitors. I think people were afraid to bother her at home, perhaps feeling a bit uncomfortable being there. While they were visiting, I walked down to the nurses' station to chat with her nurses to get out for a break. They had a list posted at the nurses' station for those patients who did not wish to have any heroic measures taken if they should die. They referred to this as a no-team, which means that the resuscitation team would not be called should they go into cardiac arrest; in other words, they would allow the patient to die. I noticed that my mother's name was not on the list, and so I asked them to check with her doctor and make sure that the orders were put back on so that would not happen. Mom had decided that when she first found out about the cancer and did not want to be revived should that time come. If the good Lord decided to take my mother, I didn't want anyone to interfere.

IN THE PALM OF HIS HAND: MY JOURNEY OF FAITH

I returned to the room to find Aunt Mary getting ready to leave. I gave her a hug and thanked her for coming. She expressed the feeling that my mother's dying was very hard to accept. I told her it was very difficult and that maybe someday we'd understand it all.

Mom had drifted off to sleep. Occasionally, her hand would reach out, and I wondered what she was reaching for. God, how I wish I understood and knew what to do. It seemed so senseless for her to lie there suffering so much. The nurses assured me that they would call me if anything changed, and they urged me to go home and get some sleep. She seemed so peaceful, just lying there sleeping, so I kissed her good-bye, whispering "I love you" in her ear, and turned to leave.

Monday, January 23

Night was not a comfort for Mom. She was in a lot of pain today. They removed her catheter, but no one knew why. It was so difficult for her to get up to use the bedside commode, and I didn't understand this reasoning. They had her scheduled for the CAT scan of the tumor. I wished that they would leave her alone and just keep her comfortable with the pain medication, but I supposed that they had to at least try to do something for her. I wished that the good Lord would be merciful and take her away from all this misery. I had left my children at the neighbor's house, and I wondered if I should have a standby plan in case Mom died. Died. Oh God, how I wished it would be soon. I could not bear the pain in her eyes, but she never complained out loud. Perhaps she should let it all out. Why not? Where was it written that we must suffer in silence?

They arrived to take Mom down for her scan. I walked down with her and then left to find my friend Paulette who worked at the hospital as a secretary. Her dad died from cancer a year ago just before Christmas. I could imagine how hard that holiday must have been for them. She invited me to join her for lunch. We passed by

IN THE PALM OF HIS HAND: MY JOURNEY OF FAITH

my dad on the way there. He seemed a bit frustrated over something but wouldn't say what.

During lunch, we talked about the frustrations surrounding a death such as her father's and my mother's from cancer. I was glad to be with someone who understood my fears. I told her I was so scared at the thought of Mom dying, not knowing if I had the strength to face that time when it comes. Her dad had slipped into a coma as a result of contracting pneumonia, so when he died, she was not able to speak with him as she would have liked. I guess I hoped that Mom would be alert at the end. I don't know. No matter how it happened, I knew it was not going to be easy. I thanked her for listening, and we parted company. As always, she assured me that she would be praying for me. I needed all the prayers that I could get. That was the only thing that would get me through all of this.

When I got back to Mom's room, she was eating a bit of lunch. Dad was not there, and she did not know where he was. He apparently left for lunch. Mom's friends Helen and Gordon stopped by and wished her well. The pastor from the cathedral stopped by and said that he was surprised to find her here. He had just been to see her last week at the house, and said she seemed to be doing pretty well. They talked for a little bit, and then he prayed with her and gave her his blessing. I thanked him for coming, and he smiled, then left. I was glad to see that the church was here for her.

I left the room to make some phone calls. Mom was sitting up in bed fumbling with the newspaper. She kept picking it up and looking at it and then setting it down. I wasn't sure if she was really coherent. When I came back into the room, she was holding the phone up to her ear. I asked her who she was talking to, but she didn't answer. Finally, she said she was calling Father Stan, who had just left moments ago. She couldn't tell me why she was calling him, just that she was calling him. Oh well, I guess she was getting a bit confused. Finally I convinced her to give me the phone, and when she did, there was no one on the line. I hung it up and noticed she had drifted off to sleep again.

I left at three-thirty to pick up my children and wait for Ernie to get home so that I could go back up to the hospital. Dad told me that I should stay home. At first I was unwilling to leave Mom alone, but I changed my mind and decided to stay home with my family. I bathed the kids and went to choir practice instead. I had enjoyed being a part of the choir, and it had been a helpful diversion for me during this time, one that I desperately need. About 9:26 I started crying. A sudden wave of anxiety struck, and I was thinking that Mom must have died. Thoughts raced through my mind. I was sure that I would have been called, but nonetheless, I still felt anxious until got home and found that it was a false alarm. Before I left church, I lit a candle for Mom, offering up some prayers for her and crying for the two of us. I planned to go up to the hospital again in the morning. "God, please grant us a peaceful night," I prayed silently.

Tuesday, January 24

I stopped by church to receive communion before dropping Emily off at Ellen's house. Receiving the Eucharist had given me the strength I needed to face these difficult times. Ellen and Emily were such a pair. I was just so grateful that I had such a good friend who would take care of Emily for me at a moment's notice.

    I left for Joliet and decided to run a few errands before going up to the hospital. I bought myself a pretty suit-type dress, just in case I needed one soon. I felt that none of the outfits at home was appropriate funeral attire. Perhaps I was preparing too well, but I had to keep myself going somehow.

    I arrived at the hospital to find that Mom was very confused. She insisted that my husband was trying to reach me, so I called him at work, but he said that he had not called looking for me. Oh well. Mom drifted off to sleep. She didn't seem to be in as much pain, for which I was relieved, but she was definitely in her own little world.

    Aunt Mary was there when I arrived, and flowers were delivered, sent by two of her daughters who had been up to see her last night. They didn't think that Mom remembered that they were there, but she said she did. Dad arrived, and Mom greeted him by saying, "Oh,

I see you've got a day off from work." He reminded her that he had been retired for ten or twelve years now, to which she replied, "Oh, so you do have a day off!" It was kind of cute and funny, but sad too. It didn't bother me except when she was aware that she was confused. Then I felt bad for her because it frustrated her that her mind was not clear! We had a nice visit, though sometimes her mind wandered off to other times in our life. Mom sat up for lunch and was also able to use the commode today. She seemed to be improving.

After I got home, I talked to her doctor, and he seemed to think that she was stable. He also thought that maybe she might go home in a couple of days. I was unsure about this idea because I couldn't imagine Dad handling things at home with her present condition of not always being in the present time. I decided to call the hospice office and find out more about the home care available for Mom in her present condition. I learned that due to Medicare regulations, we could only send Mom to a nursing home for a limited stay. I didn't know if I could handle taking care of Mom at our house either. I knew that it would be hard on all of us, but I felt like there was no other option. I asked her doctor whether Mom was on any medications that he felt she could stop taking, especially in her present state of health. He seemed to think that, other than pain medication, the other medications for her arthritis and heart were really not beneficial to her and could be stopped, but it was a decision that I felt she should make if she was able. It bothered me though, and I had to wonder what was the best for her now. I called my sister-in-law and asked her what she thought of removing any unnecessary medications, but she was not sure either. We agreed to discuss it later.

Sleep was not comforting. I tossed and turned all night, thinking of why God just didn't end this suffering for Mom. Emily awoke during the night, and I sat quietly rocking her in the living room, stroking her soft blonde hair, silently crying to myself, wishing that Mom could just be healed or freed from this dreaded nightmare.

Wednesday, January 25

I awoke at 8 a.m. and dressed for church. I arrived in time for the prayers of intercession. I couldn't pray my prayers out loud. I was asking God to grant Mom her final rest. After Mass I spoke with Sister Mary Pat and told her of my concerns about Mom and the possibility of removing her from unnecessary medications. I cried because I did not want to have to make that choice. She said she understood and offered me comfort. Somehow, just that offer of comfort made me feel more at peace. I expressed that I wished it were easier for Mom to die. I felt as though God was not listening, and I didn't want to have to make these decisions myself.

I left to go back home, and I phoned the hospital and checked on Mom. Her doctor was there, so I was able to speak with him. He told me that he had removed Mom's heart medication and all medications not having to do with comfort and pain control. I was relieved. The Lord had heard my prayers, and I did not have to make that decision. After speaking with her doctor, my brother called, and I relayed the information to him. I also told him that the doctor said Mom was much worse and would definitely not be going anywhere at all. It was the sign we had waited for, one telling us that the end was nearing. At last we could focus on making her as comfortable as possible for however long she had left. The doctor seemed to think that she would not last a week. A week. Seven days. It was hard to imagine that she would be gone in that time. I wondered if I could truly imagine her dying. I dismissed that thought and prepared to go to the hospital to be with her.

When arrived at the hospital, I found Mom to be in a sort of daze. I inquired as to why she was on oxygen, and they told me that it was to make her more comfortable and not so anxious.

Lunch arrived, and Aunt Mary was here to see Mom, so I asked her to help Mom with lunch. Mom only seemed to want dessert. I couldn't blame her. She and her frail ninety-pound frame deserved to be able to eat dessert first if that's what she wanted. After lunch was over, she drifted off to sleep awhile. She seemed to be daydreaming a lot today. Although she was not always in the present time frame, she did recognize me. At one point, she asked if she could call the funeral home for the funeral arrangements. This startled me, so I asked her whose funeral arrangements she wanted to find out about. She replied, "Dad's." I told her that my dad was fine, but perhaps she was thinking of her dad's funeral back in 1953. Mom looked at me and asked me what room she was in. I told her the room number; then she asked if the baby was next door. I asked her whose baby she was referring to. She meant mine. I told her that Emily was now three and a half years old and no longer a baby. She closed her eyes and drifted off to sleep.

When my pastor Father Ted came in to see her, Mom opened her eyes and said hello. He asked her if she had seen Jesus yet. She said at first that she wasn't sure, but then said that she had, but He was a different species than us. She also said that she thought she saw her mother last night. She thought she was dying last night. She had a difficult night, which probably accounted for her sleepiness today. Father Ted blessed Mom and prayed for a happy death for her. I

IN THE PALM OF HIS HAND: MY JOURNEY OF FAITH

thanked him for coming, and he promised to keep me in his prayers, too. I knew that many were praying for me, and I was so grateful because knew that it would help me get through all of this.

After my pastor left, I sat gazing out the window at the gray, drizzly day. It was a very dreary and foggy day, a miserable sort of day. As I sat there staring out into space, I prayed once more that the Lord would take my mother gently and soon. I wanted my mother to be at peace, not lying there miserable and without a will to live. It just didn't seem fair for her to have to lie there and suffer.

I heard a familiar greeting from one of my mother's dearest friends here at the hospital, Sister Dolorita. She came into Mom's room to check up on her and say a prayer with her. She told me that during the night, she and my mother had recited the Memorare together during the time that she thought she was dying. I didn't even know the prayer myself, but I was told that Mom recited it perfectly. Bless her little heart. Mom was quiet, sleeping peacefully. Every once in a while, she would reach out and then look startled. I asked her what she was reaching for, and she said, "The steering wheel."

"Where are you going?" I asked.

"To church," she replied.

I told her that she was in bed, and she said that someone could drive her there. I just smiled to myself and agreed with her. She began talking about the new baby, and as far as I could figure, she was thinking of her niece down in Texas who just had a baby boy. I assured her that we would probably receive a picture soon. I glanced up at the clock, noting that the time was now 4:40 p.m. Mom had been in and out of consciousness. She talked of many different times in our lives. She talked about one of my brothers running home from church and how she was going to spank him when she got home. She had taken many trips in her imaginary car, and I guess I was glad that she was not totally aware of the present. She didn't seem to know that she was talking silly, whereas yesterday she would get frustrated when

115

she realized that she was talking silly. Perhaps the Lord was protecting her in His way from her suffering and pain. I wondered if she even knew why she was here. I just hoped that when she went, it would be easy for her.

My cousin Judi and her husband stopped in, so I took a break while they were visiting with her. Mom recognized Judi and spoke to her husband. She said that she had met him a few times, which we weren't sure whether she meant that jokingly or not. I was so glad that they came up to see Mom, and Judi offered to help out in any way that she could. I said that I would let her know, that perhaps I might need her to stay with Mom if she hung on much longer than a few days. I was grateful that when the chips were down the family would step in and help.

The phone rang, and it was Mom's brother Jack, who was in a hospital in Chicago with bronchitis. They didn't talk too long except to exchange "I love you" to each other. He felt badly that he could not get down to see Mom, and I'm sure he realized that this could be it for her. I was sure that he felt that life had caught up with both of them and had not been too kind to either of them. I hoped that he would get well and hang in there for a while.

Aunt Mary arrived to stay with Mom while I went to an appointment that I made with the tax man. I didn't really want to go, but I knew it was best to get this matter out of the way now while I could. Dad had been in earlier, but I did not tell him of my intentions for staying overnight with Mom in the hospital because I knew he would get upset. Although he was not able to do it, he could not understand my need to be with Mom and not leave her alone. Mom was sleeping peacefully, almost like the night that Grandma died. Her breathing was shallow and quiet. Perhaps she would just slip away like Grandma did. I left Aunt Mary with a number to where I would be and told her that I would return as soon as possible. She didn't mind. She had brought her knitting along to keep her busy.

IN THE PALM OF HIS HAND: MY JOURNEY OF FAITH

She had always brought her knitting along for as far back as I could recall. She was always busy doing something creative for one of her family members.

When I returned, I found Mom sound asleep, and Aunt Mary was busy with her knitting. We spoke quietly and talked about the time when her husband, Jim, died. He was Mom's brother, and Mom was very upset when he died. She was pregnant with me then, and the grief took its toll on her during that time. Shortly after Jim died, her father died. My first few months of life were spent in a grief situation. Perhaps that accounted for my all-too-serious look at life most of the time. It was nice to share these thoughts with my aunt. I was glad to be able to talk about death with someone I felt I could trust to understand my feelings. It is so nice to know that when you really need your family, they are there for you. You just have to be willing to reach out to them and ask for help. I thanked her for staying with Mom, and she said anytime. After she left, I settled down for the night ahead, hoping that it would be peaceful.

I prayed for our heavenly Father to come and take his child Dorothy home soon, in peace and tranquility. "Good night, Mom, God bless you, and I love you," I whispered in her ear.

Thursday, January 26

I finally dozed off around 2:30 a.m. in the family room lounge down the hall from Mom's room. I curled up on the couch and tried to get some sleep. Mom was resting quietly when I went down to the lounge, and I just couldn't get comfortable sleeping in the recliner. The room was a bit chilly, too, so I asked for a blanket to cover the air vents to try and make the room a bit warmer for both Mom and her roommate. I slept fairly well and awoke about 6 a.m. I walked down to Mom's room to check on her and found her sleeping peacefully, so I left to go down to the chapel for morning Mass. I lit a candle for Mom and placed it by our Blessed Mother, asking her to watch over Mom and be with her today. I guess I should go home for a while this morning and get cleaned up, change clothes and come back later. Today Mom should have some visitors to keep her busy, as it was the twenty-fifth anniversary of the great move of the hospital from its former location to the present one, so there would probably be a lot of people here that Mom knew.

It was a very dismal day for a celebration, with the skies gray and dreary, but the rooms were well lit with florescent lighting. I couldn't believe that it had been twenty-five years since the hospital

IN THE PALM OF HIS HAND: MY JOURNEY OF FAITH

moved. I remember that day and what a big production it was. The move was the big news of the day in the papers, and Mom was a part of that day. Mom had been assigned to the new intensive care unit as an assistant head nurse. She had to attend classes to learn how to read the new heart monitors, and she did well, finishing at the top of her class with many nurses who had just graduated from training. Sister Theresa had picked Mom for the assignment, knowing that she was getting one of the best nurses around. Mom and Sister Theresa were classmates at the school of nursing back in 1933, and although she rose to the administrative position at St. Joseph's, she had highest regards for my mother's dedication and service to the hospital and its patients. I was so proud of my mom for her accomplishment and the fact that she was much older yet not afraid to try and accomplish that feat by going back to school when she was in her mid-50s.

I recall the blizzard of '67 when it was impossible to get any-where, much less to work, but Mom volunteered to go in, and an army jeep came out to the house to take her to work. The staff was short that day because the roads were impassable. While we stayed at home and enjoyed the winter wonderland, Mom was busy caring for the many ill patients in the ICU.

The skies finally cleared. I departed for home around 10 a.m. so that I could get home before Emily left for preschool. Todd was home from school with a virus and upset stomach. When got home, he seemed pretty chipper, so while Ernie took Emily to school and paid some bills, Todd and I played some games. Once sat down, I realized just how tired I was and decided that I had better take a shower and clean up before I fell asleep.

I straightened up the house a bit and spent some time relaxing with my son. My best friend, Donna, called around 4 p.m. to check on Mom's condition, and she offered me her sympathies, hoping somehow that I'd manage to get through all of this. Donna and I had a very special friendship, one that I had always been able to count on. When we were children, I often thought of her as my sister. I admired her for her many achievements, especially when she pursued a career in nursing like my mother. No matter how far apart we were, we were always close in our hearts. After we talked, I said good-bye to the family and departed for the hospital with a bag packed for overnight.

I found Mom to be quite alert when I got back. She had quite a bit of company this afternoon, including seven nuns who she was especially close to, including Sister Theresa Ettelbrick, the former administrator. Mom shared some good memories with all of them, and I was sure that her spirits were lifted. Another dear friend, Sister Camilla, spoke with Mom, and Mom told her that she would say hi to another nurse, Marge, so Sister Camilla told me later that she knew Mom was ready to die.

While all the nuns were there, one observer inquired of my aunt whether Mom was herself a nun.

My aunt just laughed and said that they were just good friends of Mom's.

Aunt Mary told me that she and Mom took a trip to Ohio this afternoon, so I knew that she was still hallucinating. I guess it was better this way than to watch her suffer with the pain. Her roommate had a horrible day, suffering with uncontrollable pain.

I had wanted to bring the kids up to see Mom, but had been afraid that the woman in the other bed might scare them when she screamed out with her pain. I hoped her doctors soon got that pain under control, as I could barely handle the screams myself. Once, she was so racked with pain that I thought she would leap right out of her bed. How awful it must be for her and her family as her cancer, a tumor on the spine, was not discovered until just before Christmas, and now she was close to death.

Maybe our Lord would be merciful to both the patients in this room and give them rest in heaven. Mom ate a good supper tonight

IN THE PALM OF HIS HAND: MY JOURNEY OF FAITH

though, so all that visiting must have improved her appetite. I called my children and let them speak to their grandma, and she was so glad. She kept telling me how proud she was of me and my family. I just wished that she would be around to see my family grow up. I hated the thought of them not having my mother around.

Grandmas are special people, and it was hard to imagine their childhood without her here. As I looked at her though, I realized that it would be selfish of me to insist on her living in this pain and misery. As much as I hated to lose her, I could not bear to watch her deteriorate day by day. I wondered how I'd handle her death, whether I would survive the pain of this loss.

I had grieved, but the grief, I was sure, was nothing compared to the final loss. God, help me to be wise to your mercy and allow the Spirit to guide me in my days ahead. It seemed to be the time now to truly trust our Lord, for she is truly in the palm of His hand now. I kissed Mom good night and tried to settle down for some sleep. I was very tired since I didn't sleep well the night before, so I fell asleep easily on the recliner in Mom's room.

Friday, January 27

I slept from about 11 p.m. to around 1 a.m. when Mom awoke and asked for a drink of water. She was not comfortable in that bed. Her body ached all over, and she was feeling nauseated. She said that she had some phlegm in her throat but she was unable to find the strength to cough it up, so I finally had to get her nurse to suction it out for her. I could feel the sensation of gagging when the nurse inserted the tube down her throat to clean out the mucus, and I felt the urge to gag myself. The nurse remarked that there really wasn't much mucus in her throat, but Mom seemed relieved to have it out anyway. After the nurse left, I moved my chair over next to her bed so that I could be closer to her. I took her hand in my hand and stroked it gently, trying to reassure her in the best way that I knew. She seemed to be very nervous this morning, almost as though she was anticipating some sort of action. The nurse brought in a suppository for the nausea and a nerve pill to help her to relax. She turned and looked at me and told me how glad she was to have me there by her side. She was very uptight and told me that she felt like she was climbing the walls.

IN THE PALM OF HIS HAND: MY JOURNEY OF FAITH

I reached into my purse and found my prayer book and began reciting a few of the prayers that thought might comfort her during this time. I felt odd, not really sure of myself while I was praying for her aloud. I guess it was because we never really prayed together as a family should. When I thought back to my childhood, I was sure that I must have said my nighttime prayers, but I didn't recall the times that my parents may have sat on my bed while I said my goodnight prayers. How strange it seemed not knowing those memories. It made me wonder if my children would recall their own memories of their bedtime prayers. When I listened to Emily reciting the Hail Mary, it brought tears to my eyes, or to Todd who had learned that prayer plus the Our Father, Glory Be, and the Act of Contrition. I couldn't imagine them not remembering these moments when they grow up, but it may happen that way. Now as I prayed with my mother, I wished that I felt more secure so that I could really say what was in my heart, but I hoped and prayed that she knew and that God knew and heard those prayers that I could not seem to put into spoken words.

Mom seemed more comfortable and smiled at me, my thanks for praying for her and helping her to relax. The night seemed so long; the hours passed by slowly until finally I was able to doze off a bit around 6 a.m. We woke up again around 7:30, and after that I tried to doze on and off, but she needed sips of water and some comforting. When the breakfast trays arrived, I got up for the day and tried to feed her a little breakfast, but she was too tired to eat and only wanted to sleep. The aide came in to give her a bath and change her gown. She even washed Mom's hair, which I know made her feel better.

During the night when Mom was so nervous, she said that she wanted to go to God, so I told her that it would be soon. She was really anxious last night, and it scared me. I just hoped that she felt assured with my presence there for her and that I helped her in some way. My cousin Judi would be staying with her that night, and if Aunt Mary could come stay with my children the next night, I would be back to stay with Mom once again. I wondered what the children thought about my absence from them so often, and they had not been able to come up and see their grandma. Soon, I hoped to bring them up. Right now, I thought that the other patient might scare them with her uncontrollable outbursts from the pain she was suffering. I hoped that they would get her pain under control soon, because it was very disturbing for both my mother and all of us who had witnessed her suffering and pain.

My cousin Mary Ellen walked in around a quarter after eleven and informed me that she was there to relieve me. I thanked her and gathered up my belongings. Before I left, I showed her where everything was and asked her to give my mother frequent sips of water. She said she would take good care of Mom, so I kissed Mom good-bye and told her that I would see her later. I saw my dad as I was leaving and said hello and good-bye.

He generally would come up around the same time each day, at noon and five o'clock. I stopped by the grocery store and picked up a few items that we needed. I went by Mom's house and found her nurses' hat and her pins that she wore on her uniform when she was working. I looked in her closet for the dress that she told me that she wanted to be buried in, and found that it still had the tags on it and had never been worn—a very pretty blue floral dress—and the bottom part of the dress was pleated. I thought to myself that she would look beautiful in it, but realized that she would be wearing it very soon.

Last night I thought she was going to die. When she was so anxious, it scared me, and I was not sure if wanted to be with her when it happened again. I wanted peace for her, but I was not sure I was ready for the final act. I felt as though I was only going through the motions of living, not really fully aware of life itself. I was afraid of how I'd feel when the numbness wears off. I was afraid of feeling the reality of her death and how it would affect my outlook on life. I wonder if I'd be able to find the reasons for living and whether life did have a purpose. I could not deal with this now. I felt that I must get home and try to have a normal as possible day with the family, catching up on the laundry and other household chores, until I could finally go to bed and, I hoped, sleep. It had been a very long day.

Saturday, January 28

God, how good it felt to sleep all night long. I didn't even get out of bed until after 9 o'clock. We all had breakfast, and then I did a couple loads of laundry. Todd had a bad cough but seemed to be doing all right. He and Emily watched cartoons all morning while I did some housework. I called to check on Mom, and my cousin said that she was awake from around 1 a.m. to around 3 a.m. but did all right after that and slept till morning. She ate a good breakfast and seemed to be more alert today than she had been in the past week.

During the course of the day, Mother had several visitors and was quite alert for all of them. I was planning to go to the hospital after my husband left for work, so I prepared a nice dinner for all of us, a chicken divan recipe that we all enjoyed, complete with salad and biscuits. Emily helped me cut out the biscuits with a heart-shaped cookie cutter which made her happy.

I persuaded the children to stop their wrestling by talking them into playing a game of cards with Aunt Mary. After they settled down a bit, I took Emily in and bathed her and got her into her pajamas, then left instructions for Todd to do the same. Thank goodness that he could take care of himself when it came to some of these tasks.

IN THE PALM OF HIS HAND: MY JOURNEY OF FAITH

He was growing up so fast, and Emily was not far behind with the "I could do it myself" routine. They both had been terrific throughout this whole affair with my absence for such long periods of time. My heart was torn at which end I should be, but I didn't want Mom to be alone at night especially because she was fading so fast, and I didn't want her to be alone or afraid. I hoped they would not resent this time but would accept this part of life with their childlike understanding and tolerance.

When I arrived at the hospital, I found Mom to be very tired. Apparently all her visitors today wore her out. She was even too tired to eat supper and slept most of the night. I let her rest and visited with her roommate's family, sharing my popcorn that I brought up to the hospital. I also brought up a wine cooler for myself, and being a good mother, Mom told me I should not be drinking in the hospital. I laughed to myself and told her that I was old enough to have a drink and that I would not be going anywhere afterward, so not to worry about my driving and drinking. She seemed to be getting a little anxious again, so I moved over to her side and sat next to her. The nurse came in and gave her some medication to calm her nerves and something for nausea again.

I heard voices out in the hallway and thought I recognized one of them, so I poked my head out to see one of our bishops talking to another patient's family members. I waved at him when he saw me, and he came over to see me. Bishop Karrer was surprised to hear that Mom was in, and stepped into the room to say hello. He mentioned that he had tried to visit Mom last Saturday but that no one was home, and he did not realize that she had been taken into the hospital. He spoke kindly to Mom, offering up a prayer for her for a happy and peaceful death, and then he gave her his blessing. She beamed with such radiance at the sight of this man, and I was sure his words of comfort touched her deeply. He told her that she was now on the cross with Christ, and it was not in his power to have her removed from it. I realized now that she was truly suffering with Christ, and the only way out of this was going to be her death, but we didn't know how long she would have to hang on that cross before that occurred.

When he left, Mom was a little more assured, but I could see this pain and suffering had taken their toll on her physically, and I could see how tired and weak she truly was. I wished she did not have to surfer any longer. I stroked her hand and brought out the prayer book once more to recite some prayers to comfort her. She turned to me and smiled, thanking me over and over for being here at her bedside. I was her rock, her strength, and I was there. I just told her how much I loved her and how I wished that her suffering might soon be over. Thoughts of many childhood memories floated in and out, but I knew that I could not tire her with conversations of the past. I just hoped and prayed that I had been a good daughter to her and that somehow I would find the strength to get through all of this when it was all over. I asked her one question, and her reply was interesting. I asked her if she still wished God would touch her now, heal her from this cancer, and restore her to health. Her reply was a definite "Yes."

Sunday, January 29

When morning arrived, the day began in a dismal fog. Mom slept pretty well last night. I touched her feet only to discover that they were icy cold, a sign that the nurses told me indicated that the end was nearing. How I wish I knew when. I sat down and looked over her funeral liturgy once more, making corrections for the printers before dropped it off at their house. I asked them to print it in a rainbow of colors, as Mom loved all the pastel colors best. I hoped that many of her friends would be able to come to her funeral, especially her classmates of the Class of '29. I would like her funeral to be special, just as she was special. I hoped that it would be soon. She had gone down so, just since yesterday. She was growing weaker each day.

I went downstairs to attend Mass at the chapel in the hospital. I prayed that our Lord would come to take his daughter Dorothy home to Him soon. Mom had been taking communion each morning, but her mouth was so dry that I had been giving her a drink of water after she received communion so that she was able to dissolve the host. I started doing this after one morning when I returned from morning Mass to discover the host was still in her mouth, as her saliva was not enough to dissolve it on its own. Doing these small seemingly insignificant tasks for her seemed to make her appreciate my presence with her. How I wished that I could do more for her, yet I must stand by and watch her die a little each day.

Mom's hospice volunteer was coming up to relieve me, and then my cousin would again spend the night tonight. In the morning Mom's friend Aileen volunteered to stay with her so that I could remain at home with my family until Monday night when I would return to spend the night. I explained to Aileen that Mom did not seem to want to talk too much. She had been very quiet, and I did not want her to tire Mom with endless conversation. She understood and was grateful to have the opportunity to stay with Mom and care for her very dear friend. I was glad for her too because I know how much Mom had meant to her, especially when she was going through the RCIA process and Mom was her sponsor. She was almost in tears as she spoke of the friendship she and my mother had enjoyed. I knew that she would be saddened deeply at the loss of my mother. I decided to leave when I saw that Mom was quiet and someone was with her. I tried to go home and remain calm in the midst of her impending death.

Monday, January 30

Mom had a pretty good night, according to my cousin Judi. Aileen came in around 9 o'clock and relieved her. Aileen said that Mom was very quiet except for some small conversation. She thanked Aileen for being with her and caring for her like she did. I knew it meant a lot to her to spend some time alone with Mom. I was sure those memories would help to sustain her after Mom was gone.

Ginny, her hospice volunteer, came in around lunch, and so did my dad. My cousin Mary Ellen came in, and so did Aunt Mary.

I decided to stay home until Todd got home from school so that we could all come to town together. We stopped at the mall, and the children spent their allowances on toys. We then came to the hospital to see Mom. Todd and Emily were very quiet. They were happy to see both Grandma and Grandpa. They brought Grandma a picture that they had colored together, and we hung it up on the wall so she could see it. The patient in the next bed had been quiet all weekend, and I was told that she had lapsed into a coma. Thank goodness, there were no outbursts of painful yelling while the children visited their grandma. Ernie and the children stayed about half an hour, just long enough for grandma to get hugs and kisses and to exchange their "I love yous." They left for dinner with Dad at their favorite fast food place, and I remained there with Mom for the night.

Around 8 o'clock the aides came in and settled Mom down for the night. She fell asleep quickly and was very quiet. We didn't get much chance to talk tonight. It seemed as though we didn't have much time alone. The night was relatively quiet.

Tuesday, January 31

Morning was beautiful. I woke around 6 a.m. and walked down the hall to stretch my legs a bit while Mom was still asleep. I met the night nurse out in the hall, and she told me that the patient down at the end of the hall had passed away this morning at 5:15. She had been in there for over thirty days with her family standing by waiting for that moment to arrive. I had met several of the family members and was amazed at their sense of camaraderie for each other. They were practically living at the hospital, bringing in food for the family members there, enjoying the company of one another. It seemed so hard to believe that their vigil was finally at an end. I would miss seeing them, but I was sure that it was a relief to them to finally have their loved one out of pain. I asked the nurse what she died from, and she told me that she had the same type of cancer as my mother. I asked her then if she thought that we, too, might be in for such a long wait, watching my mother die day by day. She seemed to think that Mom might only last another week at best, but who knows. Only God for sure.

I told her that Mom rested quite well this past night, and I was even considering whether or not to spend the night tonight. If I did, that would mean two nights in a row for me which would be difficult. She seemed to think that once Mom was settled in for the night, she would probably not even notice if I were gone. They had been giving her a tranquilizer at night to help her relax, and the morphine had been increased and given to her every four hours, so her pain hadn't been getting ahead of her like it had been before. I decided to think about it and asked her too if Mom might be transferred to the private room now that it had become available. She told me she could not see any reason not to move Mom, so I was glad that we would finally be able to have a room to ourselves, a little more intimacy than we had now. Mom was on 40 mg of morphine every four hours now, which I thought was a large dosage, but the patient next to Mom was on that much per hour, and the lady who just passed away was on 400 mg per hour. I could not imagine the immense pain that she must have been suffering through, and I hoped that Mom would never have to endure that amount of pain before she died.

I walked back to the room to say good morning to Mom. She was feeling a bit nauseated this morning, so she was not too eager to have breakfast. I decided to wait for the priest to give Mom communion so that I could offer her a drink to help wash the host down since her mouth was so dry. After she received communion, I went down to the chapel for Mass. My prayers were not specific that morning, but when we said the Our Father, I emphasized the part about "Thy will be done" and really asked our Lord for His will in my mother's condition. I wondered whether or not the candle that I lit for Mom the other day would still be burning, imagining that when it went out, then perhaps Mom would pass away. I dismissed those thoughts as fantasy and continued to celebrate the offering of the Mass. I left Mass with a sense of peace and returned to find Mom awake and thirsty.

Breakfast arrived, so I tried to get her to eat something. She opted for some 7 Up and ice cream instead. I teased her, saying that

IN THE PALM OF HIS HAND: MY JOURNEY OF FAITH

she must feel like having a party, but I was sure that the soda and ice cream settled her stomach better than oatmeal or cornflakes. I told Mom that she was going to move down the hall this morning, and she seemed pleased. I even decided to go out to the mall and buy her a couple of nightgowns to celebrate the occasion. I pulled open the curtains to show her the beautiful sunrise. The skies were clear and bright. The weather had been relatively mild all winter long, but today was an exceptionally beautiful day. I thought to myself that it was a beautiful day for the Lord to come take Mom home to heaven, then promptly dismissed that thought and turned to see her smile.

I bent over and kissed her on the lips, whispering, "I love you," and she whispered back, "I love you, too." She smiled that beautiful Irish smile, and when she did, I found myself filling up with tears, so I turned away. I did not want her to see me cry. It was too much of a beautiful day to cry. I turned back to her once I regained my composure, and tried to make light conversation. Her voice was only a whisper, but she was alert and knew where she was and what day it was. I kept her comfortable and offered her occasional sips of water to keep her mouth moist. I put some Chapstick on her lips to keep them moist too so that they wouldn't crack and bleed. When she first arrived here, her lips were so dry that they were peeling, but now they were soft and moist, so I was pleased that the therapy was working.

Dad called. He was coming up this morning instead of waiting till noon. I decided that I would run out to the mall when he came. He thought it was foolish, but I went anyway, arriving forty-five minutes before they were due to open. I never bothered to look at my watch until I got to the mall. I left there and ran over to the discount drugstore to pick up a few items I needed at home. I picked up some black nylons to go with the black dress I bought last week for Mom's funeral. I guess it was time for that now. As I walked through the card aisle, it dawned on me that Valentine's Day was only a couple of weeks away. I decided to buy my mother her card early, just in case she was not with us then. I usually tried to keep the costs down on greeting cards since they were outrageously priced, but a beautiful card caught my eye, and I read the verse and knew that I had found the right one. It was expensive, but I knew it was probably the last card I would be able to give my mother, so I didn't hesitate at all. When I left there, I drove back to the mall which had just opened. I looked around to try and find a gown in Mom's size, but the selection was very limited. I finally found two very pretty pastel gowns and charged them.

With my mission completed, I drove back to the hospital, knowing that Dad was probably wondering where I was, and I was hoping that Mom and Dad might have had some time to talk to each other or that Dad at least talked to her and expressed his feelings to her, but I would never know that for sure.

I returned to find the nurses in with Mom, and Dad standing out in the hall. He was anxious to leave, but said he would return later. He told me that Father Stan from their church was in but was unable to see Mom since the nurses were in caring for her. He promised to return later. When the nurses came out, I went in, putting on a cheery smile, and proceeded to show Mom the new gowns I had just purchased for her. She managed to smile a little and even chose which gown she would like to wear for the day. I took the valentine card out that I bought her, signed it and dated it; then I went over to her side and proceeded to read it to her.

The outside of the card read, "For You, Mother—What is a Mother?" I don't know who wrote the verse, as it was not signed, but it read like this:

> A MOTHER is that someone
> Who is always close at hand
> To give advice when needed
> Or to simply understand.

IN THE PALM OF HIS HAND: MY JOURNEY OF FAITH

A MOTHER gives you all her love
No matter what you do
And even when you make mistakes,
She still believes in you.
A MOTHER is a cheerful smile,
A word of sympathy,
And everything that makes a home
The nicest place to be.
A MOTHER is so wonderful
No words describe her worth
And, Mother, it's for certain
You're the dearest one on earth!

The inside verse was not so appropriate, with its wishes for happiness and joy, but that poem said all the words I could not say on my
own. Of course, I cried while I was reading it, but she didn't notice,
as sometime during my presentation she had drifted off to sleep. I
hoped that she had heard the verse, as it was so much of what wanted
to say to her. I bent over and kissed her forehead and told her that I
loved her. I placed the card on the table alongside the flowers that she
had received from her nieces, and walked over to the window to gaze
out at the beautiful sunshine day.

My daydreaming was interrupted by a familiar voice belonging
to Mom's dear friend, Sister Lorraine. She walked in and sat down on
Mom's bed, and Mom awoke to her gentle voice. She spoke briefly
to Mom, asking her how she felt today, and Mom responded that
she was not feeling the best. Sister Lorraine listened intently; then
she held Mom's hand while she offered up a prayer for Mom, asking
that our Lord be merciful and take her servant Dorothy home soon.
I choked back my tears and thanked her so much for coming in. She
turned to me and smiled, saying that it was her pleasure and that she
would see Mom again the next day.

137

We hugged each other, and she told me to take care of myself. I said that I would try but that it was not easy. I tried to be upbeat, telling her that Mom would be moving down the hall which I hoped would cheer her up a bit. Sister smiled at me and told me that I was such a good daughter. I thanked her, but I felt that I was doing what only seemed natural to me.

Thursday, February 2

My mother was dead. The last two days were a blur. She died at a quarter past twelve., just about thirty minutes after Sister Lorraine had been in. Shortly after noon, Mom began having difficulty breathing. Her nurse had given Mom an injection of morphine for the pain, but it was not able to control her pain this time. She looked at me, the pain so very obvious in her eyes, and said, "Help me." I ran out into the hall and told the nurse there to come help me calm my mother down. Mom's nurse was busy, so the nurse that I talked to ran into Mom's room to see what she could do to help her. She spoke gently to Mom, telling her to relax and try to think of something beautiful. She held Mom's hand while she talked, and I stood by her side, my heart racing and my whole body trembling with fear. "This is just like the other night," I thought to myself.

Fear was taking over my emotions, and I tried not to show it toward Mom. The head nurse and Mom's nurse finally came in, and her nurse gave Mom a tranquilizer, but it seemed to be too late. The head nurse turned and looked at me and asked me if there was someone I wanted to call because, she told me straight out, "Honey, this is it—your momma is dying."

I couldn't believe what she had just said. I held onto my composure long enough to tell her to try and reach Sister Lorraine, to call my dad and see if my aunt was in the hospital working. The aides who had been so good to Mom came in, preparing to bathe her, and instead stood by as moral support while I watched my mother die. The ward clerk came back to say she could not reach Sister Lorraine, so I asked them to call Sister Dorothy from the pastoral department at the hospital. All the while this was going on in a matter of a few frantic minutes, Mom was struggling to regain her breath. The nurses had elevated her head so that it would be easier for her to breathe, but it did not seem to be helping.

By this time I was in tears, telling her that I loved her, but it was okay for her to go. I told her not to fight it, just to let go and let God. "Our Lord has you in the palm of His hand," I reminded her. Sister Dorothy appeared and put her arms around me. I turned to her and sobbed on her shoulder; then I turned back to Mom. The clerk came in again, telling me that Dad said that he'd be here in twenty minutes, which drew puzzled looks from the nurses and staff. I wiped away the tears and said, "That's okay. He's giving her time to go." Sister Dorothy offered up a prayer for Mom, asking our Lord to take her gently. All the while I kept telling her to go toward the light, to let go and take His hand.

The nurses kept telling me how great I was doing, but I was scared to death. I was looking death right in the eye, and it was not a pleasant sight. It wasn't peaceful, like grandma's death, but then my mother never did do anything in an ordinary and peaceful fashion. The nurse who was checking for Mom's pulse said that it was getting fainter. I turned to Sister Dorothy who was standing next to me and cried on her shoulder once again.

The nurse announced that there was no pulse. I turned back to Mom, told that I love her, and kissed her good-bye. Then her body heaved its final breath, and she was gone. It was as though her spirit had left at that moment in time and space. I placed her hand down on her chest and held her gently in my arms. I cried uncontrollably now, not trying to hide or hold back the tears. My aunt came in just moments after Mom passed away. We held each other tight, and she told me how sorry she was. I told her it was okay. Mom had won. She no longer had to endure the pain and suffering of the cancer. I only hoped that she lost consciousness of the feeling of pain at those last moments of life. She fought so hard. Surely, she did not really want to die. She did not want to quit.

Dad arrived just a few minutes after Mom passed away. He did not want to deal with it and spent time fussing with the items in the room. Finally, I spoke to him and said, "Dad, your wife has just died. Will you please stop what you are doing and tell her good-bye?" He laid down what he held in his hand and turned his attention to his wife. He went to her side and picked up her arm and told her that he loved her, then kissed her goodbye.

I walked down the hall to the lounge area and used the telephone to call my family. Ernie was surprised that Mom had died. I guess he wasn't expecting it to happen in the middle of the day. He said I should take all the time I needed to make the arrangements, etc., and we agreed to tell the children when I got home about their grandma's death. I then called my church to tell them the news and found out that Bishop Karrer, who had been to see Mom the other day, was there having lunch. I asked to speak to him, and at first he did not know who I was, until told him my maiden name. He then offered a more personal note of sympathy, saying how surprised he was and sad, too, at her death.

I went back to the room and found that Dad was talking to my brother on the phone. I spoke to him briefly, noting that he was having a hard time talking. Finally the confusion died down, and we said our good-byes to the nurses who had cared so well for Mom while she was here. I was saddened at the thought that Mom never did get the chance to move down the hall or wear the pretty pink gown I had bought her. I thanked them all, and we left to go to the funeral parlor to make the final arrangements.

When we arrived at the funeral home, we were greeted by one of the directors, and he offered his message of sympathy. H ushered us to the back office where we sat down to discuss the time we wanted for the funeral and to select a fitting casket for Mom. I handed him an obituary that I had written for Mom. He noted that it was rather lengthy and would therefore probably cost a lot of money. I said I didn't care because she deserved to have her story told. He took us into another room that was filled with all sorts of caskets, ranging in price from one thousand to ten thousand dollars. He showed us a very pretty one in blue, saying that it was also available in white, which he thought would be very fitting for Mom, since she was a nurse. The price was modest but not inexpensive. I persuaded Dad to take the one he was suggesting. It sounded so lovely, and I wanted Mom to have something beautiful for her final rest.

I was under complete control all the while, making rational statements and wondering whether I was crazy for not being upset. I selected the prayer cards for my mother. They were the same ones that we had for my grandmother. I wondered later whether I had chosen the right ones, but it was too late to change it once it had gone to the printers. We left there and drove to the florist; then we drove back to his house. I stayed for a while, but then I had to get home. I was anxious to see my family, but I wondered how I was going to tell them that my mother had died. On the way home, I saw a bright blue star up in the heavens, thinking to myself that this was my mother's place in the heavens, her star. I thought too that this might be a way of telling them about their grandmother's death. Emily was the first one that I told this theory to, and she accepted it with her innocent childlike understanding. Grandma's star. That

IN THE PALM OF HIS HAND: MY JOURNEY OF FAITH

seemed to appease her, and I was glad. Todd was a little more subdued, perhaps because he understood that Grandma had died.

It was ten after twelve, Thursday, and we were awaiting Danielle's arrival so that we could leave for Joliet to go to the funeral home for the wake. Kathy Kay and I attended Mass this morning at St. Mary's, and Kathy was impressed with the care and concern of my fellow parishioners who came over to us after Mass to offer their sympathy for Mom. We came home and got the children up and ready to go to town. My neighbor came over to express her sympathy and offered to help out in any way we might need. I thanked her for her support, and we exchanged some quiet conversation. Finally, we were all ready to leave, so it was decided that Emily would go with her uncle John and aunt Kathy to keep Stacie company going to Grandpa's house. Todd remained with us to await Danielle's arrival.

Yesterday, Uncle George flew in early in the morning for Mom's funeral. He arrived at Dad's before noon and took a little rest. I left home to finish the errands necessary before the wake and funeral took place. I stopped by the printers to pick up Mom's liturgy booklets and was surprised to learn that there was no charge. They were in lieu of flowers. I gave Marge a hug, and the tears streamed down my face. I thanked her for their generosity, then left to go to Dad's to pick up her wedding bands and to see Uncle George. I invited him to come along with me while I dropped off the liturgy at the cathedral and to stop by the funeral home with Mom's rings and her rosary. He gladly joined me on my errands and was most pleased to meet the dear friend of mother's, Sister Lorraine.

She was most impressed with Mom's liturgy and promised to take care that they were delivered to the church in time for her Mass on Friday. She was pleased to meet Uncle George, noting the striking resemblance between him and my mother. I told her that Helen Talbott would read one of the readings and asked her to read the other. I had also wanted another friend of Mom's to read the prayers

143

or intercession, but had been unable to reach her. Sister Lorraine said that she would try to get a hold of her for me. I thanked her, and we left. I then felt a bit guilty at not having a role for Uncle George to participate in his sister's funeral Mass. I decided to ask him to lead us all in a prayer at the funeral home before the wake began. He was most agreeable to that idea.

The phone rang, interrupting my daydreaming. It was Dad looking for John, and I told him that he had left. He handed the phone to Uncle George, and as we were speaking, John arrived. I informed my uncle that John had made the final reservations for lunch following the funeral. We decided to limit it to family and close friends. Just as we hung up the phone, Danielle arrived. She had stopped in Kankakee due to slight car problems but arrived just fine. We exchanged greetings and hugs, then loaded up in our car and left for my dad's.

Dad had enough food to feed an army, and we were all hungry. He had said that he did not want anyone to send food, but he finally realized that they would do it anyway, so he gave in. Sending food was a way of extending sympathy on the part of your neighbors and friends, and I thought it was wonderful how the neighbors and friends responded at the need. As soon as we all had our fill of the delicious array of food items, we gathered up our families and headed to the funeral home. I was hoping that Mom would look nice, and I was worried how the children would respond to seeing their grandmother lying motionless in the casket. Thoughts ran wild through my mind, only to stop when we arrived at the funeral parlor, and it was time to face my mother once more. This time, however, would be different. She was really dead, and I was going to have to face that fact here and now. I guessed I was ready. I hoped that I was.

It was quiet in the funeral home. The aroma of fresh flowers permeated the air. I could pick out the scent of the carnations, Mom's favorite flower. The children were nervous. Todd clung tightly to my

IN THE PALM OF HIS HAND: MY JOURNEY OF FAITH

hand. Emily was the least reserved. She ran right up to the casket and tried to get up so that she would be at the same level as her grandma. I walked up to her side, and she spoke to her grandma as though she were alive.

"I love you, Grandma," she said excitedly. "I'm going to miss you, Grandma." When I looked at Mom, the tears began to flow quietly down my cheeks. She looked beautiful. Gone were the signs of struggle and pain. She was at peace. She had won. Todd brushed up against my side and buried his head in my arms.

I held him tightly; then he spoke to Grandma telling her that he loved her. He was a "little man" acting so grown up for his tender six years of age. Stacie was a little nervous. She spoke quickly and quietly like a little mouse, telling her grandma that she, too, loved her and would miss her very much. She then ran back to the couch and lay there nervously giggling to herself while her mother sat by her side to reassure her and herself.

Each of us came over to Mom's side, noting that everything was just beautiful. The flowers were gorgeous. Dad had changed his order from having just a few pink roses to a beautiful arrangement of pink carnations, which I am sure would have pleased Mom.

Uncle George was to lead us in a prayer, but before long the people began streaming into the parlor, and time escaped us. I turned around to see Aileen, Mom's dear friend, entering the parlor room. Kathy and I walked over to her and escorted her up to the casket. She was taking this really hard, and we knew that she needed our support. We stayed with her while she paid her respects and shared a tear with her, and then we embraced, our sorrows now uniting. Soon the funeral home was filled with people. Time seemed to stand still.

Friday, February 3

We awoke early to begin to dress for the funeral. The weather had turned colder. I decided to wear pants and dress the children warmly. January had been unusually warm, without much snow or rain. Now the air had that cold crisp snap to it, the kind that makes your nose tingle with an unpleasant sensation. We were all very tired, since we stayed up late last night sharing fond memories and going over the day's events. I hardly remembered going to bed, but we must have slept, although my body still ached for more slumber. Soon, however, the nerves were responding, and I began to get anxious to leave for the funeral home. Somehow, we all managed to get ready and leave by 7:30 a.m. so that we could be at the funeral home in time for a last good-bye before going to the cathedral.

I gave my last minute instructions to the funeral director for the flowers and Mom's personal effects. Many friends arrived at the funeral parlor to give their regards and support for our family. My best friend, Donna, arrived, and we greeted each other with an embrace. We tearfully made our way up to the casket and held each other's hand while we spoke of Mom and how peaceful she looked. She was sorry that she couldn't make it last night, but she had not

IN THE PALM OF HIS HAND: MY JOURNEY OF FAITH

been feeling well and wasn't sure if she would make it at all. But she did, and I was glad. Her friendship had always been important to me. We had shared a close bond since we were small children. I had always admired her intelligence and compassion. Our friendship knows no boundaries whether we see each other often or not. When we were together, I felt a secure sense of acceptance, something not often held by other friends or family. Her family played an enormous role in my life as a stabilizing factor in my turmoil and strife or my childhood.

Her mother and father offered a sense of comfort when my home life was beyond my control or liking. It seemed fitting to have her father as one of the pall bearers for Mom. He was like a second father to me, always offering a smile and trying to help out when times were difficult at home.

At 9 a.m. the funeral director came in and led us all in a prayer for Mom. Then he instructed friends to pay their final respects and leave to arrange their vehicles for the trip to the church. When we were left alone, our family went up for the final good-bye. Kathy and I stayed till last, holding each other and crying, mostly for ourselves. I placed the nurse's hat at Mom's side and laid the single red rose on her shoulder. I placed the button that Todd had given his grandma for Christmas inside the casket with her. It said that she was an "Extra Special Grandma." The director removed Mom's rings and her necklace and handed them to me. He also gave me her rosary which I then gave to Kathy.

He placed inside the casket the small pillow of carnations which was from the grandchildren.

Then he asked us to say our good-byes as it was now time to go.

I had not wanted to touch my mother, because I remembered how cold my grandmother had felt when I touched her, but I couldn't bear not to touch her, to kiss her one last time. I wanted to embrace her forever so that I would not have to let her go. I bent over

147

her, kissed her gently on her forehead, and tearfully said good-bye. I pressed two fingers to my lips, kissing them, then placed them on her lips as our final kiss good-bye. As we turned and left for our cars, I dared not look back as I did not want to see them closing the lid on the casket, forever sealing my mother from my view.

As the procession found its way to the cathedral, I played with the carnation I had taken from one of the bouquets of flowers at the funeral home. The air had turned bitterly cold, and a few flurries of snow began to fall. Mother always hated snow and cold weather. I was glad that she did not have to put up with it anymore. We lined up our cars in the driveway at the cathedral, waited inside the large lobby while the pallbearers removed the casket from the car and placed it on the cart. Our family and friends gathered around us, and we lined up ready to walk ceremoniously down the long aisle to our seats. Mom's friends Gordon and Helen were there handing out the copies of the liturgy, and everyone remarked how beautiful they were. My friends had indeed done a splendid job. They were a sort of mint color with gold lettering and with the Isaiah 49 symbol of the child in the palm of the Master's hand. At the top were the words "In loving Memory of Dorothy Kenney Busse, born June 10, 1910, passed to Eternal Life January 31, 1989." Inscribed below the palm were the words from Isaiah 49: 15, "I will never forget you. I have carved you in the palm of my hand." Everyone was surprised that I had prepared this all by myself. They all remarked how beautiful they were and how proud Mom would be to see what a fine job I had done.

The pews were filled with many people, both family and friends. Most everyone was a familiar face, but some were known only to my mother, and I was sure she would have been pleased to see so many people come to share her funeral Mass. After Father Stan recited the opening prayers, they clothed the casket with a white cloth, symbolizing her baptismal gown for her journey home to heaven. He blessed

IN THE PALM OF HIS HAND: MY JOURNEY OF FAITH

the casket, sprinkling it with holy water, and then the organist began to play the opening hymn "Be Not Afraid." We made our journey down the aisle, greeting those who extended their hands in sympathy toward us. My father was having a difficult time, so I was glad John stood next to him to show his support.

After we were seated, I sat staring at the white cloth, recalling a story that my dad's sister had just relayed to me last night at the wake. She spoke of the time when she was giving birth to her first child. During that time she actually died for a few minutes due to a nurse giving her too much ether. While she was in that state, she recalled seeing what she believed to be our Lord, dressed in a dazzling white robe, standing on a white cloud. Between her and the Lord was a golden bridge linking the cloud she was on to the one our Lord was on. Behind our Lord were many people, all dressed in white robes, with happy faces on all of them. Around their waist were cords of gold. Some of the people she knew, like her mother and dad who had died when she was very young. She could hear the beautiful singing of the birds, and then the Lord spoke to her, saying that it was not yet her time, but if she chose to remain, she could stay. She replied that she felt that she should return, but did not know why. He then spoke to her and said, "Woman, return from whence you came." The next thing she remembered was the sound of her baby crying, and she knew why she had to return. By her telling me that story last night, I felt assured that Mom was truly in heaven smiling down at us during this time.

The funeral was beautiful. Helen read the first reading from the book of Wisdom, chapter 3, verses 1–6. This was followed by the psalm "I Lift Up My Soul." Sister Lorraine read the second reading from Romans, chapter 14, verses 7–12. Father Stan read the gospel; then he gave a most fitting homily, depicting the marriage of my mother and father as "two strong personalities." I was amazed at how he seemed to pinpoint their relationship in just a brief encounter with my father a couple of days ago when he stopped by the rectory to see him. When it came time to read the prayers of the faithful, my uncle rose to take over for my mother's friend who was unable to be at the funeral due to a fall she had taken the day before. I was so glad that Uncle George would have a part in my mother's Mass, and he did a splendid job of reading the prayers that I had written for the occasion.

During communion I found myself breaking down in tears. Perhaps it was the selection that the organist was playing which I had chosen for this occasion, "On Eagles Wings." As I turned to my husband, he squeezed my hand to let me know it was okay. All of us were in tears, but it was okay to cry. After communion, Father Stan read the remarks I wrote to my mother for me, as I knew I would be unable to do it without breaking down.

For My Mom

Dorothy Busse—wife of Ted and mother of John, Doug, and Kathy—had one unfailing trait: her constant faith. A faith so strong that even the cause of her death, cancer, held no triumph over her. She accepted it as her cross and fought a gallant fight. We are grateful that God allowed us time to understand and to heal and to prepare for her passing. As we look back over the time we have had since her diagnosis, we see a woman who was brave enough to look death in the eye and say, "You have no hold on me." Her confidence in God never faltered. Her biggest prayer was for her family, that we might be united through her death. I believe she will continue to pray for us. She taught us to be strong and to face things with confidence. I know the Lord held her in the palm of His hand, and so did she. Even when we forget Him, He never leaves us.

Mom, mother, wife, and sister, may you have joy and peace and rest and suffer no more. We ask that the Lord be merciful to you and take you this day to paradise where all tears will be wiped away and joy is infinite.

Good-bye, Mom, we love you!

Soon the Mass was over, and we were once again processing down the aisle to the waiting vehicles to make our final farewell at the cemetery. By now the snow storm had gained momentum, and the flurries were flying about us. We gathered at the burial site and listened while Father Stan led us in our final prayers. He told me afterward that we were a most unusual family. I think he, too, was impressed with the liturgy and the sense of organization that it displayed. I took his remark as a compliment, which I am sure is what he intended. We left the cemetery to go to the restaurant where we were joined by our family and friends for a final tribute of this memorable occasion.

Monday, February 6

As I looked back over the last few days, I felt peaceful. The wake ended at 9 p.m. It seemed strange to me that the bulk of the crowd came between 3:00 and 5:30. After 8 p.m. the funeral parlor quieted down considerably. My husband and my sister-in-law left around 7:30 to take our children home to bed, since we were going to have to rise and shine the morning of the funeral. So many of my closest friends—like Pat and her husband, Bill, and Kathy, who lost her grandmother the same week that I did in 1987—and old neighbors and friends of my parents came by to pay their respects to my mother. Her ICU daughters—like Pat and Theresa, fellow nurses that Mom shared many good times and memories with—came in with tear-stained faces. We hugged and embraced each other; our loss seemed to be a link between us all. Some of the people, professionals that Mom knew, had to introduce themselves to me as I did not know all the faces that came in.

My family was a great source of comfort. My brother and I shared the responsibility of greeting all the wonderful people who stopped by to pay their respects to our mother. Dad was great. He talked to many people and shared some wonderful memories with

IN THE PALM OF HIS HAND: MY JOURNEY OF FAITH

them that night. I hoped they saw the side of Dad that cared deeply about Mom, even when he didn't always allow that side to be seen. My cousins and their families stayed almost the entire wake, greeting other relatives. Although we would like to see more of them during happier occasions, it seemed as though these were the times that drew us together. My dear childhood friend Paulette; her son, Eric; and her mother came by, and I was glad that I had not left to go for a bite to eat as I had when my grandmother had died when I ended up missing her altogether. She understood what we had been through; her dad had died just barely a year ago from pneumonia following his last cancer treatments. She had been a dear friend since childhood.

Marce and Russ and their daughter Kim came by and expressed their grief and sentiments. Marce and Russ had been like second parents to me, always there when I needed a lift emotionally and always inviting me to be a part of their family activities. I had many wonderful memories of childhood because of the wonderful neighbors like them who opened their doors and their hearts, allowing me a place to be free and to feel at home. Their daughter Donna and I had shared a friendship that has also spanned our lives since childhood. We were not close in distance, but in our hearts there were no boundaries affecting our friendship with each another. Her sister Kim has also been a great friend. We had shared many memories together, and I was appreciative that she was able to come down from Chicago for Mom's wake and funeral. At first we weren't sure if Donna would make it, as she was ill. But she came on Friday, and I was so glad to see her. I doubt that I would ever have a friendship with anyone as open and caring as Donna had been to me.

My parish staff members came out in force. Father Ted and Sister Mary Pat and Sister Remi came together. They were all out "vanning" from wake to wake. Many people had died this week. Father Ted and I approached the casket together and offered up some private prayers for Mom, which made them very special for me.

Shortly after that, Bishop Karrer arrived. He lead those present in a recitation of the Memorare, Mom's favorite prayer, which I had printed on her funeral cards. I was caught off guard because I did not know that prayer by heart, and the thought occurred to me to pass out the funeral cards to the people in attendance, but I did not want to make a scene. I did know that I was not the only person who did not know that prayer. I had resolved to learn it by heart. I imagined that Mom must be proud to think that the bishop, whom she had known since he was a young priest at the cathedral, came to her wake and lead us in prayer.

The crowds came and went. Many of Mom's former classmates came from the Class of '29. When I saw Mom's classmate Helen, I cried out with excitement because I had been told that on the day Mom died, Helen was leading the noon prayers at the cathedral seniors' meeting and had asked that the Lord take Dorothy, my mom, home to heaven because she felt that Mom was ready to die. Little did she realize the impact of her prayers until later when she realized that my mother died at 12:17 p.m., just a few minutes after her prayer! Many of the people stayed a while to visit with other friends who they met there. My dear friend Rae came by, and she met up with a former classmate with whom Mom had worked. I felt the love and concern of so many people that night that I knew Mom would be pleased. Many people asked for my brother Doug, who chose not to come back for the funeral. I offered no explanation for his absence, and thought someday he would live to regret that he was not there.

I have only one regret since Mom died. I regret not taking a photograph of her in the casket. As morbid as that sounds, I wish that I could see her once again, not just in my memory. She looked so beautiful, and I wish I had captured that on film. I have a picture of my grandmother in her casket which was taken because one of her granddaughters was out of town when she died, and Aunt Mary

IN THE PALM OF HIS HAND: MY JOURNEY OF FAITH

felt it would help make it easier for her to accept Grandma's death. I have a few pictures of other members of my grandmother's family at the time of death, taken mostly by my aunt Sadie, who was a photographic nut. Perhaps it was a fear that the other family members would think I was crazy or that was being like Aunt Sadie that I chose not to photograph Mom, but I do now regret that decision. I also wish that I had chosen the pictures of the saints for Mom's funeral cards, as she was so very fond of the saints of the Catholic Church, but I am sure that she has forgiven me for not doing everything perfectly.

After the funeral, John and his family left the funeral luncheon to visit our uncle Jack who had just been released from the hospital with severe bronchitis. He had come home on Thursday supported by a portable oxygen tank. He was unable to come to Mom's wake or funeral. My brother was anxious to see Uncle Jack because of his illness, and since they had to return to Colorado the next day, they decided to go on Friday. His family had a nice visit with both Uncle Jack and Aunt Nelly. Uncle George was there too, prior to his departure back to California that night.

Saturday, John, Kathy, and Stacie visited one of Mom and Dad's old neighbors, Hazel. She cooked them a lovely dinner, and they had a wonderful time reliving fond childhood memories of when my brother was a little boy. It began to snow in the afternoon, so John and his family left Hazel's and stopped by Dad's to say good-bye. They also made a stop by the gravesite to bid their final farewell to Mom before they headed back to our house. The snow was falling steadily now, and John feared that a winter storm was brewing, so when they returned to our house, they said their good-byes to us and decided to try to make as much headway as possible before the storm hit hard. Our children hugged their cousin Stacie, and we tearfully said good-bye. It had been an emotional few days, full of both sadness and rediscovery for my brother and me, who were able to share one of the most important events of our lives. We relived many memories in those few days we were together. It was good for us to be able to open up and talk about matters of the heart. I knew that we shared a special moment, one that would remain with us throughout our lives.

The weekend was a busy one for my family. My church celebrated its centennial with a special liturgy. Both Todd and Emily had a special part in the liturgy. (Dad joined us for Mass and sat with my children while I sat in the choir loft.) During the presentation of gifts, Todd and Emily and their grandpa carried up the wine, water, and a ciborium, presenting them to Bishop Imesch, who presided at the Mass. I thought of how proud Mom would be at seeing them, and I knew that she was probably watching over it all from a heavenly view. Many fellow choir members had come to me and offered their sympathy, which made me feel good, although I was still in a trance of emotionless feelings. I had not yet cried for my mother. I was still in a state of shock.

Tuesday, February 14

The time was 4:42 a.m. The night had been long. I could not sleep due to the terrible cold or pneumonia that I seemed to have. I had been tossing and turning all night and even allowed myself the luxury of a few tears for my mother. Or perhaps they were more for myself. I had been sick since Ash Wednesday, just about a week. On Friday I had to force myself to be well enough to take Emily to the doctor for her ears—again. The doctor took a look at my throat, but I was not sick enough to be diagnosed with anything.

By Saturday I was couch-bound with two children who had the run of the house for the day until their dad returned from work that night. The house was a mess, but I was too sick to care. As long as they entertained each other, I was content to curl up on the couch and sleep, between food and drink requests from the children. I resolved to make them more independent for small matters when I recovered from being ill. I thought about seeing a doctor but could not find one who was in and had an opening. One office suggested that I come in on Monday, but I replied that I would either be dead or better by then. Instead, I suffered with a 102-degree temperature, chills, cough, and headache throughout the entire weekend. I thought I was better on Monday. I even did laundry and cleaned up the house while my family went to town and saw a movie.

In that early morning hour, I realized that this was a serious illness because my chest was so tight I could hardly breathe. That was a very scary feeling. It brought back vivid memories of Mom, on her last day, when she could not catch her breath. I wondered if I was experiencing the same feeling that she had just before she died. I could only hope that she lost the conscious feeling of suffocating at the very end. I was scared too, thinking that perhaps I had what my mother had, and that was what caused her to die. I was wondering in these wee hours of morning if I was going to die. My thoughts turned to my mother, and I kept wishing that I could see her just one more time. I hoped that she would appear to me in a dream so that this emptiness inside could be filled once more with the sound of her laughter, but I sadly realized that it might never happen.

My stomach was growling, so I decided that perhaps I should get up and have a snack. As I wandered downstairs to the kitchen, I tried to decide what I should have to fill the empty feeling inside. I decided on toast with jelly and a cup of herbal tea. I popped a slice of bread in the toaster and put on the teapot. My attention went back to the toaster when the bread popped up, and it was then that I felt the presence of my mother with me. The toast came out burned black, my mother's favorite. Somehow the toaster browning control was set at the darkest spot, one that I never use. I felt then that Mom was there with me, watching over me, protecting me from above. To me the toast was that sign, silly as it might seem.

So why was I sick? They say that grief takes many forms. I was so busy taking care of things that I forgot to take care of myself. I guess that this was our Lord's way of saying that I should slow down and take the time to cry for my mom. After all, she was well worth crying over. I decided to allow myself to shed a few tears, even though

IN THE PALM OF HIS HAND: MY JOURNEY OF FAITH

it made me feel even worse physically. I would call the doctor's office just as soon as they were in this morning.

Todd and Emily had Valentine's Day parties at school today. As much as I would have liked to attend, I knew that I was not able. I explained this to Todd since I was supposed to help at his party, and he assured me that he understood. Yesterday I watched both of them make valentine cards for their parties, and it was amusing how Emily would correct her dad if he made one of her letters the wrong way. Finally I had to get out the letter guide so that he could make the letters the same way her teacher did at preschool. Todd was a marvel of efficiency. He wrote all of his cards by himself, all twenty-seven of them! I was amazed at how far he had come since the beginning of the year. If losing my mother had taught me anything, it had taught me to be thankful for the many good years that we shared and to cherish my children while they were growing up, hoping that they would cherish me when I grew older, and perhaps sick and weak.

I had written almost one hundred thank-you cards for people who sent flowers, memorials, and Masses. I wished that I could thank all those who simply attended. It was wonderful to know how much she was loved and admired by her contemporaries. I only hoped that I could begin to fill her shoes, not that I wanted to take her place, but to leave my mark somewhere in this life—that when I died, I might be remembered as being one who tried to build, not destroy, the foundations of life and its principles as my mother did. No matter what my mother faced in life, she strove for what was right and just. She was a quiet giant, one who did many good things without sounding the cymbals or rousing the band. She was dedicated to life. She believed in the right to life for the unborn. She believed in it enough to help by contributing her time and her professional knowledge for the advancement of the Birthright office. Many times she was called upon to deal with the doctors, to help these mothers who had nowhere to turn except to these charitable organizations which helped provide mothers with a sense of hope in these dismal days of destruction of the lives of the unborn. She also lent a hand at the Mission Club at her church, donating time to help make cancer pads for the terminally ill. It seemed so ironic to me now. She enjoyed life despite the problems that she faced. She had friends and loved ones who kept her going despite the hardships she endured. She loved and was loved by everyone that she knew. Those were the shoes that I would like to fill. I hoped someday to publish this diary, and perhaps I could call it *In the Palm of His Hand: My Journey of Faith.*

Tuesday, February 28

Fourteen days passed since my last entry. Since that time I had been very ill. I found out that I had Influenza B (the *B*, according to the doctor, was for very, very bad!), and I also had bronchitis. I thought I had recovered about a week ago, but suffered a relapse after I had been out doing the grocery shopping and trying to catch up on things around the house.

I came down with it worse than before, almost ending up in the hospital with pneumonia. I had to call upon my dear aunt Mary to come down and take care of us for the weekend while my husband worked. She cancelled her plans for the weekend and came to my rescue. On Saturday my friend Sister Mary Pat took me to the hospital for a chest X-ray. I was thankful to have such good friend. I was afraid that my symptoms were just psychosomatic, since they seemed to be the same symptoms that Mom had suffered those last days of her life. The body ache, the fever, the chills were the same as she had when she first went into the hospital. Perhaps I was just reacting to her death by developing the same symptoms in my mind.

The doctor assured me that I was really ill and that the symptoms I had were real, not imagined. Now that I was ill, I realized that this was how my mother died. She died from the effects of the flu, not from cancer. She died trying to catch her breath, probably because she, too, had bronchitis, which was why her chest X-ray was clear. Neither of us had pneumonia; we just had this horrible flu. I even caught it from her when I kissed her on the lips the day she died. It was like a kiss of death. Somehow, though, it all made sense to me now. If the cancer had truly killed her, I believe her pain would have been much worse, and her death would have been even more difficult to endure. Even though her death was a hard memory for me to deal with, I think our Lord spared me from a more intense death which I believe the cancer could have produced had she not caught the flu and died from it. I was put on strict bed rest for two weeks. I was not to do anything or go anywhere.

Sunday my dad's sister, Aunt Bernice, and her daughter Carol and my dad came down for a visit. Aunt Mary cooked a splendid dinner for all of us, and we had a pleasant visit. I was so tired. I wondered how long it would be before I felt alive again. I still had not cried much for my mom. Soon, I hoped, soon.

Friday, March 3

Sister Mary Pat called to say that she would be over this afternoon to bring me communion since I had not been able to attend Mass at all. Todd was sick again with a sinus infection, so Ernie had to take him to the doctor. Emily and I had lunch together in the living room while she watched television. I was better, but my sense of balance seemed a bit off. Emily complained of an earache which I assumed was more a feeling of pressure than an actual infection, since she was taking a maintenance antibiotic. I offered her some chewable, non-aspirin children's medicine. I left the room to put away the medicine only to hear the cry of my daughter echoing from the living room. I rushed back to her and discovered that she had only chewed one of the tablets that I gave her, and for some crazy reason, stuffed the other one in her nose!

I called the doctor's office where Todd and Ernie were and was told to bring her right over. I was a little hesitant to drive since my sense of balance was off, but I was left with no other choice. I phoned the rectory to tell Sister Mary Pat that I would not be home after all, as I had to take Emily into the doctor's office for a Tylenol-ectomy! She was amused as she knew Emily was quite a stinkpot. The three of them left the doctor's office together, and I went to the drugstore for the medicines and a break from the walls of my house that seemed to be closing in on me. I had been nowhere but home for several weeks. My family left to go to the lumberyard to buy materials to build a Lego table for my son so that we could keep his Legos off of the floor so we can dust and vacuum his room more frequently, thus ridding the house of allergens that infect his sinuses. Since my illness we had not been able to keep up with the cleaning as well as we should. I stopped by the rectory, and Sister Mary Pat gave me communion, and I told her that I thought my family was tired of me being ill. It was time to get better.

Monday, March 6

I attended my first Eucharistic ministry class at Aylesford Retreat Center. It was very interesting. The class was run by Sister Joan, who has a great sense of humor. I shared some of my story about my mother, but mostly I listened and learned. I brought along my box of Kleenex, as I was on the tail end of my illness, suffering with runny nose symptoms. I sat wondering how I ended up here in this class. Clearly, God had directed my path along the way to this point in time. I was asked by my pastor to become a minister of the Eucharist so that I could bring communion to my fellow choir members at church. They had been asking for someone to do this, especially on certain church holy days such as Easter and Christmas. As it turned out, the classes I was attending would finish at Easter in time for me to become a Eucharistic minister.

I found it hard to believe that I would be a special minister of the Eucharist, as I myself had only been receiving communion again for two and a half years, after my husband and I were able to have our marriage blessed in the church after undergoing the very extensive annulment procedures from his first marriage that ended several years ago. He paid a heavy price for going through the procedure.

Our family bonds were severed for almost two or three years as a result of much misunderstood information regarding the annulment, and although we tried to explain our intentions, feelings were hurt. I thank God that Danielle, my husband's daughter, did not turn away. She still loved us and finally had accepted our reasons for the matter. I felt badly for the pain that my husband suffered for my benefit.

Unfortunately, it was the only way that I could be restored fully to my faith and be able to partake of the sacraments of the church. I credit my father-in-law for finally putting the matter to rest for the family. I was convinced that my mother prayed for us to be restored to the graces of the family because she knew how unhappy we were that things were not right between us and my husband's family. Prayer does work. I have seen the miracles that result.

After I completed the course, I would be able to bring the Eucharist to others. I had thought about attending a hospice course in the fall to broaden my understanding of the terminally ill and the effects it has on their families. Eventually I would like to visit the home-bound, bring them the Eucharist, and share a smile with them to help brighten their days. I would call upon the memories of my illness and how a visit from a friend made the difference in how the days went. My dear friend Pat brought me a coffee cup that said, "One day at a time." It has become my motto. I take one day at a time.

I felt that our Lord was calling me to this path in my life. As I listened to His call, He directed my path, making the way smooth and clearly marked. Sometimes I didn't always feel that was right for this, but the Lord gently nudged me back to His way of thinking. The classes were long, but they were only for four weeks. Easter would be here soon.

Wednesday, March 8

It was late. The kids were in bed asleep. Ernie and I were watching a movie together. I'd been drinking quite a few more of my wine coolers than normal, perhaps to try to relax my mind and avoid the thoughts that I had been carrying since Mom died. When we turned in for the night, my thoughts turned to my mother, and I began to cry. I couldn't sleep but tried to muffle the sound of my tears in my pillow so that I would not disturb my husband and infringe on his sleep. I began to sob and couldn't stop. My husband reached over to try and comfort me, but I was angry.

The worst part about crying was the plugged-up nose. God surely goofed up when He designed the nasal cavities. It was not fair that one must suffer with a plugged-up nose when you are having a good cry. It was not fair. The tears were flowing uncontrollably by now, and between sobs I was trying to tell my husband why I was crying. After clearing my stuffy nose, I tried to explain how I was angry that it had to be me who watched my mother die. Why me? Why did have to be the one who told her to go with Jesus? I wished I had known that she had the flu and had not settled for the excuse of the "dying process." I was angry that she was gone. I missed her terribly. It was two in the morning. I was exhausted but unable to sleep because I was finally crying for my mother. It had been over a month since she died. I was finally able to cry.

Thursday, March 9

My husband went to town to do the grocery shopping for me. According to the doctor who treated me for bronchitis, I was still not supposed to go out into public. I was still tired from last night, and although I did finally sleep, it was not enough to restore my reserves. I did manage to get Emily ready to go to preschool and was just about to leave when the phone rang. It was Denise, a friend from town. She called because she felt the Lord was telling her that I needed to talk to someone, and she thought she could be that someone. I thanked her for calling but had to hang up. I promised to call her back just as soon as I returned from taking Emily to school.

As I drove her to school, I debated whether or not I wanted to return home right away and call her or wait until later. I decided to call her back, as though an inner voice was prompting me to do so. We talked; I cried. We shared memories of our mothers and how much we missed them. Denise lost her mother a couple of years ago in an auto accident, so she understood how I was feeling. I told her how upset I was that my father seemed to be giving all my mother's things away too fast. I hated the thought of walking into their house and it being so empty, especially her closets that were so filled with clothes that they were about to burst. Now they would be almost completely empty.

I felt that I could not bear to see it like that. She assured me that although I did not agree with my dad, he was just reacting in his way to his grief. I was angry that I had been so sick and not able to get up to my mother's to take charge of her possessions, but I felt that there was a reason for my not being able to go there that I just didn't understand right then.

I felt much better after talking to Denise, and I thanked her for letting me share my thoughts, my fears, and for listening to me grieve, finally, for my mother. We ended our conversation when I noticed it was time to go back and pick up my daughter at her school.

I stopped by our church rectory and made arrangements to have a Mass said for what would have been my parents' forty-seventh wedding anniversary. Emily was looking forward to seeing our pastor, as she liked him a great deal and always liked to share a hug with him. While I waited for a chance to talk with Father Ted, Emily amused herself. She struck up a conversation with another of her favorite people, Scott, who worked for our church.

He showed her all about computers, and she enjoyed the attention. When my turn came, we went upstairs to the family room, where Emily made herself feel right at home. We exchanged greetings, and already the tears began to fall. Emily was upset that I was crying, and I told her it was okay. She knew that I was crying for my mother, and she stated so. Father Ted listened attentively while I talked about my anger over my mother's death, and although I wished it had not been me who held my mother's hand as she died, I felt that the Lord was calling me to deal with even more. I expressed my anger at the wasted years that my parents spent by their lack of kindness to each other, but I was grateful that my dad stood by my mother in her greatest time of need since her illness began. I knew in my heart that they loved each other, but I just wished that they could have expressed it differently over the years. I wished that it had been my dad, and not I, who was at her bedside when she died, even though I knew it was better that he was not.

The tears had begun to flow rapidly, and I confessed that this was the first day that I was able to cry since my mother died. Father Ted came over to my side and hugged me. I cried on his shoulder, telling him that I missed my mother so terribly much. It hurt so deep down inside that she was truly gone from my life. I wondered why God had brought me to this moment in time and what purpose he had in store for me. Father Ted said that I should keep listening and following the Lord's call. I knew that I must. Even my husband had assured me last night that God must have a great purpose in store for me. I only needed to listen.

I thanked Father Ted for his time and gathered up Emily so that we could get home before Todd got home on the school bus. The tears continued to flow, but I felt better, and as Father Ted assured me, my mother was worth crying about.

On the way home I decided that I would go to town on Friday and bring as much of my mom's things home with me so that I could go through it on my own time, in my own home. I knew it was the right time to do this now.

Easter Sunday, March 26

Easter morning broke to the sound of my son's excitement over his discovery of the Easter baskets and presents hidden by the Easter bunny. His squeals of delight reminded me that I must tell that bunny to find a better hiding place next year. He came into our bedroom full of excitement, telling me what he thought was contained in the packages that he found. He ran down to rouse Emily from her slumber so that she, too, could enjoy his find. I grumbled sleepily as I tried to raise my body out of the warm, comfortable bed, not wanting to get up just yet.

As I pulled my robe about me, I reflected on the events of the past few days when I made my debut as the Eucharistic minister for the choir during Holy Week on Holy Thursday, when my husband attended services with me at our church. I was very nervous and anxious about going down to the altar for the first time, but by the Easter Vigil on Saturday night, I was more confident and assured. It was such an honor for me to be assigned this responsibility, and I thought of how pleased and proud my mother would have been if she were here to see me giving out the Holy Eucharist. She was so

IN THE PALM OF HIS HAND: MY JOURNEY OF FAITH

proud of me when I chose to return to my faith after an absence of several years.

I found it hard to believe that I had come as far as I had in my journey toward faith since my return seven years ago. I was in awe to think of the prayers that my mother must have prayed for me to come back to church. She never gave up hope for my return. She had faith in me and trust in the Lord.

How I wished that I could be bringing communion to her, but I was so grateful for the one time when I was allowed to take the Eucharist to Mom while she was visiting us for the day. She had not been able to make it to church, and I asked if someone could bring her communion at my home after Sunday Mass. I was entrusted with the Eucharist and felt then that it was such a great honor and an even greater memory of the time shared the Body of Christ with my mom. I was so grateful that I was allowed that special time, creating a special bond between Mom and myself, a bond of love for the Lord's strength through the sacrament of the Eucharist.

My head was clear now, and the children were anxious to begin their egg hunt. After the discovery of all the eggs and the opening of the gifts, revealing their special presents, we all settled down for a quiet day. I was only preparing dinner for five this year, an odd number but one that I would have to get used to. The ham was in the oven, and dinner was progressing, but somehow when it came time to get it all together, I couldn't. After all, Mom was not here. She was not here to peel the eggs or the potatoes, and there was no one to share a conversation with while dinner was being prepared as was the custom when Mom was here.

Just last Christmas, Mom sat at our table and peeled the potatoes while I prepared the main meal. She would always apologize for not being able to do anything for me, so I always made sure that I had some little task for her to do that she could do at the kitchen table. While we worked on the dinner together, we would talk about the little things that the kids were doing and how proud she was of all her grandchildren. She was so disappointed that she was not able to visit her granddaughter Stacie after they moved back to Colorado. She felt that Stacie could not understand why Grandma was not able to come out. I tried to reassure her, but already the cancer had weakened her so, that she was giving in to the feelings of helplessness that it had brought about. She cried at being less than useless, but I tried to assure her that she was not useless.

I loved her, and I needed her, especially when the trials of motherhood seemed to overwhelm me. And I would call her on the phone just so she could reassure me that I was doing okay, that I was a good mother, even when I felt that was not. Sometimes she would offer her advice on how to inspire my children to be more appreciative and less demanding, but she never pushed her ideals on me. She just made suggestions. She loved her grandchildren, all of them—from Mike and Brian, who are almost on their way to adulthood, down to my children, Todd and Emily, and their cousin Stacie. Our conversations were filled with the activities that each of them was involved with at the time. Grandma was so very proud of her family despite the heartaches that were sometimes overwhelming for her. She would just commit that heartache to prayer.

But this holiday was different. I had to prepare dinner alone, and the tears began to flow. This was our first holiday without her, one that would never be the same. My family was supportive despite the trials I endured, from getting the dinner on the table to dropping the cheesecake topping on the floor. I left the house after dinner to run to the grocery store for a few items. My excuse for leaving—to be able to cry alone, away from my children who got upset when I cried. I stopped by my church where I felt that I could be alone in my grief. The aroma of the Easter lilies reminded me of Mom, as I used to always give her one on Easter which we would then plant in our backyard to enjoy a second bloom around August.

IN THE PALM OF HIS HAND: MY JOURNEY OF FAITH

I sat in the stillness of the church and cried my heart out. I missed my mom, wondering if this ache in my heart would ever go away. I wondered if I'd ever stop missing her or if I'd ever be able to fill the void that her death left me with. Perhaps in time. I did know, however, that God truly does stand by our side to hold us up and carry us through the dark days of our grief, if we let Him. I hoped and prayed that I would follow His way and emerge refreshed and renewed in His generous spirit of love.

Epilogue

When my mother died, I thought it was a blessing. It was a blessing for her because she was freed from her suffering. I was, however, unprepared for the journey that I had to embark upon, a journey that I call faith, and I am still on that journey.

At first I coped well with her death, convinced that it was for the best but never imagined the experiences of a grief journey that are imposed upon the loved ones left behind. I was stoic at first, offering more comfort to others than what I received for myself. When people spoke to me of my mother, a sense of pride welled up inside, and I was proud to be the daughter of such a wonderful person.

These feelings remained until about four or five months after she died. Then the doubts began to creep in, and my attitudes about everything began to crumble. I moved into the desert period of my grief. I felt empty, alone, and abandoned. It seemed as though, in my mind, some members of my family and some friends disappeared. These people were no longer present in my life now, and therefore, the comfort they once offered seemed to have evaporated.

I had found the most comfort from those people who, like myself, had experienced a similar loss. That's not to say, that other friends and family members were not comforting, but their understanding was not as complete. I had found, too, that I was more understanding of those who had suffered this type of loss, noting that the hurt lay deeper than what it might appear.

In my grief work, I discovered that my priorities had changed, but not because I wanted them to. They just had. My dreams were smaller now. Instead of wishing for monetary gains—such as new cars, room additions, and financial security—I was seeking only to be accepted and loved for myself, even when I felt that I was not worthy of such love or acceptance. My self-esteem had definitely plummeted. It was way down to the bottom. I'd put on weight that I despised, and although I had access to and knowledge of the greatest diet techniques, I'd lost the motivation to accomplish this feat right now.

Through all of this, one thought had prevailed. God does comfort those who mourn. Although I'd questioned much about my life, I knew that God was there waiting for me to take His hand and guide me. I was trying to take each day as it came. If I failed that day, by God's good grace, I would have another day, another chance to try again.

The worst part of the grief journey to me had been the angry period. I would like to be, and I believe that I was, able to move out of this stage soon. I got angry over everything, especially got angry when I felt that my very sense of self, my being a mother, was questioned. I resented this because, perhaps, it is my only sense of identity.

I am not a career woman. My family is my career. When I feel the overwhelming questions regarding my family arise, my entire being seems lost without purpose. I have even entertained thoughts of departing from this phase of my life, perhaps by getting a divorce or committing suicide, because I don't feel that I am giving my family my best efforts. My husband deserves a happier wife, one who can put him back as her top priority, and my children deserve a mother who is more tolerable and not so angry all the time. I want to leave them all behind because it hurt so bad to love them and risk yet another chance of having to deal with a loss later on. It would be easier to leave and never look back—until 3 a.m., when my daughter awakens needing comfort from an earache or another bad dream.

I then realize how foolish these thoughts are. I have begun to realize that although I wish others could take this journey for me, I know they cannot. I must undertake my grief myself, and in prayer I ask God to forgive me when I am less than loving toward other people, especially my family. I realize, too, that I am not alone in my journey.

Despite the fact that I mourn my mother's death, it has opened new avenues for me: one in the writing of this book, and others in my understanding of grief, which, through the Bereavement Ministry of my church, I hope to help people in a positive way on their journey through grief. It has also been an opening for my father and me to have a better relationship, especially in light of a diagnosis of a cancerous tumor in his colon. I hope that we will gain a deeper understanding and love for each other.

I marvel at older people's ability to endure. I respect them for never giving up on life amidst the many challenges society places on us these days. Mom was one of those people. She survived. Even in her last days, when I asked her if she still wanted to be cured of cancer, her replay was simply "Yes." I believe that she wanted to live, but God chose to take her home and leave me to grope through the process of grief. Perhaps it was so that I would be made into a more compassionate and more understanding person.

I hope to gain more patience and regain love. Love of God. Love of self. Love of others. I believe God will restore my zest for life. He will restore my dreams and my goals, perhaps giving me new ones in place of the old. I am beginning to have hope. I cannot change things or people. I can only change myself, and only with God's grace. I want to become better, not bitter. All I need to do is reach out to Him and take His hand and know that I am a child of God. "See, I will never forget you. I have carved you in the palm of my hand" (Isaiah 49:15).

There is a path for everyone
To follow in this life.
At times we lag, again we run
Thru laughter and thru strife.
Each mile ahead looks clear
Till clouds come overhead
Sometimes we quake with fear
But coverage comes instead.
A day may seem a year,
A year seem but a minute,
But love will ease old fear
Till we reach life highways limit.
Each pain we feel pays interest
In life's big bank of time
Each sorrow, too, adds to the trust
To make this life sublime.

—DKB

Acknowledgements

A very important part in the production of this book which I, as author, cannot overlook is the people who either inspired me or gave me encouragement to complete this task. Without their friendship and prayers, I might never have taken those scratched out notes from my steno pads and transformed them into this manuscript. I have tried to remember all who have contributed even in a small way, and if I have overlooked someone, please know that it was not intentional.

Ernest French—my faithful, loving husband and my best friend—thank you from the bottom of my heart for all your support and encouragement. Your patience with me was genuinely appreciated, and for your endurance throughout my grief process, I remain in your loving grateful wife.

Donna Clark, for all those special years of friendship even though we are separated by many miles, we shall remain ever close in our hearts. Thank you for always being there.

Darlene Busse, one of my best friends, whom I met when she entered our family by marriage, and who has also always been more like a sister to me than I can express. Despite the circumstances that have changed in our lives, we will always remain best of friends.

John and Kathy Busse, for your love and support throughout all the years. I especially thank you for being there with me at our mother's funeral.

Dad, my deepest thanks for enduring the years of our strife and for being more of a father than I ever realized. We have been down the road or a very long journey together.

Judi Tapella, my cousin, whom I shall always be grateful to for the time you gave to mom during her last hospital stay. Thank you for being at her bedside. I couldn't have managed alone.

Mary Kenney, my aunt who helped me out when I was so terribly ill after Mom died. You gave of yourself in the care of my family, and you were such a great support during Mom's illness and death. Thank you from the bottom of my heart.

Pat Wharrie, for your loyalty and friendship and for always being so generous with your time. Your help during Mom's illness is a debt I may never be able to repay. Thank you, too, for all your prayers.

Father Ted Berst, for your compassion and listening talents and for allowing me to produce this book with your approval. Thank you for your assurance that the days that I was encountering my worst fears, I was merely going through the normal process of grief and not having an early onset of insanity. Your prayers and blessings for my mom are deeply appreciated.

Sister Mary Pat Peacock, for your comfort, understanding, and hugs. You provided me with insight into the many facets of bereavement and have become a good friend.

Scott McCawley, for allowing me to use your computer equipment and for having the patience to teach me how to use it. I owe you a debt of gratitude for your time in editing my manuscript and being honest with your criticism which enabled me to strive for improvement. Thank you, too, for reminding me than I am not older than I am, nor am I too old to accomplish my goals.

IN THE PALM OF HIS HAND: MY JOURNEY OF FAITH

Sister Lorraine Crawford, for your support that you showed to Mom. I know how very fond she was of you, and I am glad you were such a good friend.

Andy and Marce Rostello, for all those special years throughout my childhood when you stood by me and considered me as part of your family. The memories I have are wonderful. Thanks, too, for being such good friends and neighbors to Mom and Dad. I know Morn was especially grateful for all the things you did for her.

Mom's friends—Ginny Garvey, Helen and Gordon Talbot, Aileen Fredrickson—for the love and friendship you showed toward Mom, thank you for all your support.

Denise Moran, for being such a wonderful and understanding friend. Thank you for your gifts depicting Isaiah 49, which has brought me many happy thoughts during those dark days of mourning.

Paulette Cottrell, for sharing my sorrow and giving me insight from your own loss of your father. Our friendship is a treasure to me.

Deb Carlson Cowger-Thank you for your thoughtfulness by obtaining a nice new nurse's hat for my mom's funeral to be placed in her casket. I appreciate our friendship over these past many years.

There are so many wonderful people who have helped to influence this book in many ways that they are too numerous to mention, but you should all know who you are. Friends of Mother's, including Sister Dolorita, Hazel Maleski, Helen Frandsen, Sister Camilla, Mother B's daughters Edith Krystal and Genevieve Cummings, and the many classmates of the SFA class of 1929. I owe a debt of thanks for your love and comfort at the death of my mother, and for giving me insight to my mother's personality. Thank you all very much.

It's been twenty five years since I put these words on paper. A lot has changed over those years. Several of my acknowledged friends and family that I thanked have left my life in one way or another. My father, Theodore Busse, died two years after my mother passed. I cared for him in my home until exhaustion made me realize that his quality of life and mine were being severely impacted. He gladly went to a nursing home to allow me time to prepare for his passing. He passed quietly from this life on February 27, 1991, just hours after I took my children to visit him in a new nursing facility. I teased the nurses there by asking who whispered in his ear what it was costly for him to be in the facility. I was not with him when he took his final breaths, but I am so glad my children got to see him that last day. Though not a perfect man, he was my dad, and I am grateful that he loved me.

My aunt Mary Kenney has also passed, as has Fr. Ted Berst and Sister Mary Pat Peacock. Andy and Marce Rostello have also departed this life along with my mother's dear friend Aileen Fredrickson, as well as I am sure several of my mom's class of 1929 classmates.

I am now sixteen years away from the age that my mother passed from this earth. I have survived breast cancer and am happily retired with my husband in Southern Illinois. My husband is still my best supporter and friend.

My brother Doug, who I was not close to for many years passed away last year at the age of sixty-five. I regret that I never put some of the past behind us. He was a successful businessman who was always trying to make a million. I pray for his soul and for forgiveness. I pray for his sons that they will be happy and successful.

My children are grown and on their own. I am blessed to have them close in my heart. I struggle to understand life's twists and turns at times, but I never doubt the good Lord, who promises to keep me in the palm of his hand. I hope my story has blessed you, the reader, and that you too realize that God is with us always even in these troubling times.

Nativity scene painted on my parents picture window Dec 1970.

My last Christmas with my mom, Dec. 24, 1988.

IN THE PALM OF HIS HAND: MY JOURNEY OF FAITH

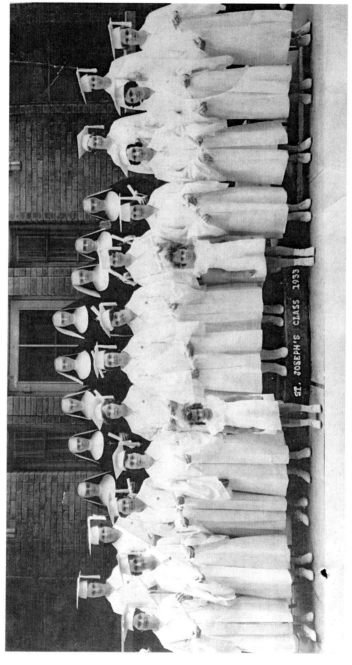

St. Joseph's Class of 1933 School of Nursing Joliet IL

Dorothy & Ted Busse wedding photo 1941

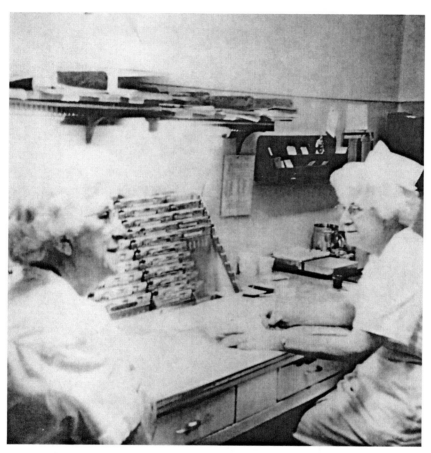
Dorothy's clever sense of humor--seeing double--a special Kodak trick photo.

Dorothy Kenney Busse late 1970's

IN THE PALM OF HIS HAND: MY JOURNEY OF FAITH

The Busse family late 1960's

KATHLEEN A. FRENCH

Satin Roses

By Kathleen French
Braidwood, Illinois

Dedicated to my mother,
Dorothy Busse, who died on
January 31, 1989.

I would buy for you a satin rose,
    one whose color never fades.
The bloom on this rose would be perfect
    for that is the way they are made.

If I had known the pain of losing you,
    I may never have agreed to let you go,
But the pain you bore was so great you see,
    that I had to let you leave.

Oh, how I wanted to ask you to stay
    yet another day with me.
But the cold winds of winter
    beckoned you to flee.

So goodbye my love, sleep tight my love,
    in Heaven where I know you to be.
I will pray for thee to watch over me,
    till we see each other up above.

I'll buy you a satin rose or two,
    to decorate your place in this world.
The kind of rose whose beauty never fades,
    just like my memories of you.

Satin roses bloom unending,
    like the tears I shed seem to be,
My expression of sadness and grief
    for my mother who was taken from me.

Poem written for my mom in the early 1990's which was originally published in Bereavement magazine.

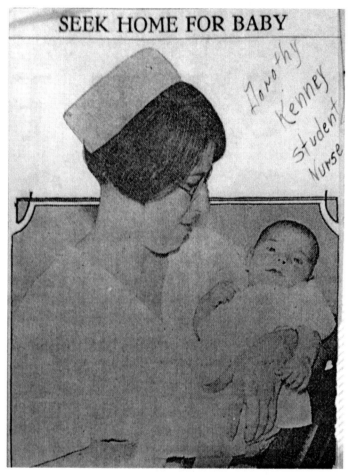

Dorothy Kenney student nurse holding a baby who was up for adoption. Photo was published in the local paper. Dorothy remained committed to pro-life issues throughout her life. Upon retirement, she began crocheting sweater sets and baby blankets for the Birthright organization in her community.

About the Author

Kathleen & Ernie French 2014

Kathleen enjoys spending time with her husband, Ernie, of thirty-seven years pursuing their bucket list of vacation destinations. In her spare time, she enjoys singing in the church choir, reading, and volunteering once a week to deliver meals on wheels. In the past, she served as a Girl Scout leader and service unit manager for eight years; previously she was involved in her parish's Bereavement Ministry during which she completed a two-year educational process in the pastoral leadership program.

In 2013, Kathleen retired from banking as an assistant branch manager in order to pursue their dreams and enjoy life. A mother of two and a stepmother of one, Kathleen aspired to publish her memoirs of the time in her life when the loss her mother's life left her with an emptiness that was never filled. She dedicates this book to her son and daughter in the hopes that they would recall the love of their grandmother who was taken too soon when they were only six and three. Twenty-five years in the making, *In the Palm of His Hand: My Journey of Faith* is relevant to anyone saying that long good-bye to their loved one.

CPSIA information can be obtained at www.ICGtesting.com
Printed in the USA
LVOW08s0550110816

499945LV00001B/103/P